Masters of Music

GREAT ARTISTS AT WORK

Photographs by JAMES ARKATOV

Text by ALAN RICH

Foreword by ISAAC STERN

Preface by NICOLAS SLONIMSKY

CAPRA PRESS
SANTA BARBARA

Printed in the United States of America.

LIBRARY OF CONGRESS CATALOGING-IN-PUBLICATION DATA
Arkatov, James, 1920-
Masters of music : great artists in action / by James Arkatov: text by Alan Rich; foreword by Isaac Stern.
p. cm.
ISBN 0-88406-314-4 : $50.00
ML87.A75 1990
780'92'2—dc20 90-36309 CIP

Published by Capra Press
Post Office Box 2068
Santa Barbara, California 93120

Distributed to the trade by Consortium
287 E. 6th Street, St. Paul, Minnesota 55101

Table of Contents

Foreword
Isaac Stern

Photographs of performing musicians, taken by a compassionate and professionally aware eye, will always be historical mementos in the enduring history of performance. This collection, including photographs taken by James Arkatov's father, Alexander, brings us an up-to-date compilation of the best of the performing artists, American and foreign, who have been regular visitors to the American concert stage. Because these pictures are chosen not only for their excellence as photographs but also for their historical content, this book can be an invaluable reference to concert activity in our day, and as years pass a warm remembrance of a host of familiar names and faces. For both performers and music lovers, and the listening audience that shares with us the magic of an artistic happening, these photographs will trigger some very special, personal moments.

Introduction
Nicolas Slonimsky

Beethoven died in 1827. Had he lived a few more years, this album might have included daguerreotypes of Beethoven at work, Beethoven fixing his ear trumpet to hear sounds that escaped him, Beethoven at the fortepiano, Beethoven in anger. Well, there may be no Beethoven, but the present album presents vivid photographs of 20th-century musicians, composers, violinists, cellists, conductors. Here is Toscanini holding a score close before him to read the notes (he was terribly myopic). He continued to give concerts in New York even when his bodily ills made it difficult for him to move around. But no matter—Toscanini still retains in the memory of musicians who played under him the image of the fabled Maestro who could do nothing wrong. Quite a contrast was presented by Serge Koussevitzky, who in his photograph seems to be imploring the orchestra to give a more *dolce* expression. Koussevitzky was the successor of Pierre Monteux as the head of the great Boston Symphony Orchestra, and no contrast could be greater physically between the two men, Koussevitzky looking aristocratic in his pose and Monteux, projecting his bodily bulk in the picture, attending to his prime business, to make the orchestra play as well as possible. Otto Klemperer was equally efficient in classical and modern music; his foible was his habit of describing his music verbally to the orchestra, causing one Italian oboe player to remark during a rehearsal in New York, "Hey, Klempy, you talka too much." Klemperer suffered a paralyzing brain tumor, but he managed to overcome this frightful affliction and actually continued to conduct after an operation. Conductors often achieve fame by their behavior toward the public and the players. Sir Thomas Beecham was made as famous by his bold utterances as by his sensitive interpretations of Mozart and other classics. Of the younger generation, there is Lorin Maazel, secure in his grasp of orchestral colors. The photographer captured Lenny Bernstein, that extraordinary musician in motion, caught literally in mid-air, weightless in a terpsichorean ecstasy.

A gallery of fantastically gifted violinists includes Fritz Kreisler, a veritable prima donna who mesmerized the audiences of the early part of this century. A virtuoso of a different type was Jascha Heifetz. He started his career as a child prodigy whose ability to produce a silken sound became a byword of perfection. A shaggy-dog story which happens to be true tells us of young, very young, Jascha at his first appearance in New York. His older rival, Mischa Elman, who attended, complained of the heat in the hall. "Not for pianists," parried his companion, Leopold Godowsky. Isaac Stern and Yehudi Menuhin are the romantic counterparts of Heifetz, while their younger colleagues Perlman and Zuckerman fiddled along in concert halls and television as if the instruments were parts of their own bodies.

Cellists are the poets of the strings, seldom arousing the plaudits of an audience by sheer display of virtuosity. But they often reach the heights of expressive power. The name Pablo Casals conjures up a vision of such greatness. In his company was the equally great Gregor Piatigorsky who added a new dimension to cello playing by his emotional and sensual style. Rapidly rising on the firmament of heavenly cellists is the already legendary Yo-Yo Ma.

Undoubtedly the richest tribe of virtuosos are pianists. This album includes photographs of such caressing giants of the piano as Vladimir Horowitz and Arthur Rubinstein, who could make the piano keys warble as the tenderest nightingale and then unleash a storm of resonant sonorities upon the keyboard. Rosina Lhevinne was a feminist of the piano, famed as a teacher as well as concert performer. Great pianistic names crowd this splendid album: Claudio Arrau, Artur Schnabel, Van Cliburn. And there are composers—the greatest of the great, Stravinsky, and Aaron Copland, a composer who made America sing.

Photographs of all these remarkable musicians and many more are assembled with artistic savoir faire by the impassionate musician/photographer James Arkatov. The album provides a visual accompaniment to the marvelous sounds of great players of our time.

Fritz Kreisler

The years go by, and the name of Fritz Kreisler has taken on a certain nostalgia. If we remember him at all, we remember most the concerts and radio appearances of his last years, made up mostly of pieces like "Caprice Viennois," and "Schön Rosmarin."

But there was more to Kreisler than that. Records, at least, survive to attest to the strength, the clean honesty of his playing: the Beethoven and Brahms Violin Concertos, ancient performances dating from the dawn of the electrical-recording era; the complete Beethoven sonatas with the noble pianist Franz Rupp; the miraculous Beethoven, Schubert and Grieg duets with the formidable Serge Rachmaninoff at the keyboard.

Every violinist since Kreisler's time owes him something. He virtually invented the modern way of string playing, the use of continual vibrato as an expressive device. A generous and dedicated musician, he played joyously wherever he thought there were people who wanted to hear him.

PHOTOGRAPHER'S NOTES

Fritz Kreisler was at once aristocratic, old worldly, and gentle. He was one of the first artists I had photographed and I had great trepidation about asking his permission to take pictures. He hesitated when I asked, and my heart sank. He went on to explain that during rehearsal he usually took his coat off—but if I didn't mind photographing him in his shirt-sleeves, I was welcome to take pictures!

Photographed with V. Bakaleinkoff in Pittsburgh, 1946.
Photographed in Pittsburgh, 1946.

Artur Schnabel

If one were lucky enough to secure a good seat and could watch Artur Schnabel up close, watch the play of the music across that seemingly impassive countenance—the sly little twinkle in his piercing blue eyes when Schubert was about to pull one of those cheeky, sudden key-changes, for example—one knew that Artur Schnabel was deeply immersed in communicating his music-making.

He lived in a narrow musical world: Mozart, the Beethoven Sonatas, Schubert, Brahms. His programs were strictly no-frills; no showy warm-up pieces at the start, no encores. He is often thought of as a cult figure, but the truth was that Schnabel's True Believers constituted an anti-cult. They came to concerts armed with the printed scores, and adored Schnabel for the way he effaced himself from the audience's awareness, serving instead as a window opening into a panorama of serious, eminently rewarding masterpieces. The window remains open, through the treasure of Schnabel's recordings, an imperishable legacy.

Artur Schnabel was never known for his lack of ego and he loved to talk about himself. At one party when he had been holding forth with a listener for an extended period of time he finally said, "Enough of my talking about myself. Why don't you talk about me?"

Photographed in Pittsburgh, 1946.

Zino Francescatti

Young Zino was pushed onto the stage by his ambitious parents at the age of five; at ten, he had already played the Beethoven Violin Concerto in public in his native Marseilles. Wisely, however, he quit the life of the child prodigy, went on to serious study in Paris, toured for a time in the 1920s with Maurice Ravel, and, in the late 1930s, made his home in New York. "If violin playing is in the way of becoming a noble art again," wrote Virgil Thomson after a Francescatti recital at Carnegie Hall, "this artist is one of those responsible for the change."

The nobility of Francescatti's art extended to his refusal to become just another virtuoso in the show-off repertory. His programs went beyond the conventional to include the music of living composers. He teamed up often with the great pianist Robert Casadesus to explore the repertory of sonatas and chamber music that de-emphasizes the performers' personalities in favor of musical values. A most musicianly violinist, Francescatti is best remembered as a musician who just happened to be a violinist.

Photographed in Pittsburgh, 1946.

Gregor Piatigorsky

To Richard Strauss, Piatigorsky was "mein Don Quixote," the composer's favorite interpreter of the solo role he'd written into his tone poem of that name. As solo cellist with the Berlin Philharmonic in the 1920s, Piatigorsky had had many opportunities to perform Strauss' eloquent tone poem. His Berlin performances had won him recognition as one of the three finest cellists of his day (alongside Pablo Casals and Emanuel Feuermann). When he finally came to the U.S. and performed Dvorak's Cello Concerto with the New York Philharmonic (in December, 1929), his fame knew no boundaries.

He settled eventually in California where he continued concertizing as well teaching generations of cellists at the University of Southern California. He commissioned new works for his instrument and participated in recordings and concerts with, among others, Jascha Heifetz and Leonard Pennario. Piatigorsky's noble, mellow way of playing, the silken phrasing, made him an outstanding performer in the grand Romantic tradition.

I met Gregor Piatigorsky shortly after he first came to America in 1929. It happened that in Russia he had studied with a Dutch cellist, Willem Dehe, who later settled in San Francisco and became principal cellist of the San Francisco Symphony and also my teacher. Whenever Piatigorsky came to San Francisco he would stay at my teacher's home, and we were friends from that time.

My father took professional photographs of Piatigorsky in 1933. He was a handsome young giant with a magnetic personality that charmed everyone.

Later on, I took pictures of him when he appeared with the Pittsburgh Symphony under Fritz Reiner, years later at a garden party at Arthur Rubinstein's, and in his final year, at his home in West Los Angeles. By then, he had undergone much illness and his physical appearance had changed greatly. But he remained to the end a warm, gracious, and generous person, loved by all who knew him.

His story-telling was legendary, but one could rarely discern whether the stories had any basis in fact—or were a romantic flight of his imagination.

Photographed with Fritz Reiner in Pittsburgh, 1947.

Photographed in Pittsburgh, 1947.

Fritz Reiner

Hungarian-born, much respected in his native land (and also esteemed as a peerless interpreter of the music of his countryman Bela Bartok), Reiner nevertheless spent by far the greater part of his career in the U.S. From 1922 on he held several American podiums: the Cincinnati Symphony, the Pittsburgh (where Jim Arkatov played under him for two years) and, for most of a glorious decade (1953-62), the Chicago Symphony. The Reiner years in Chicago are generously documented on records; they are an irreplaceable legacy.

For many, however, the peak of Reiner's career came on February 4,1949. It was the night of his Metropolitan Opera debut, on the podium for Richard Strauss' *Salomé*. The Salomé was a new, tempestuous Yugoslav soprano, Ljuba Welitsch. New York is not normally regarded as a volcanic region; that night it was. If they hadn't torn down the old house, the cheers would be ringing still.

While I was in the Pittsburgh orchestra, we had a very fine concertmaster, Hugo Kohlberg—one of the few musicians that Reiner respected. At one point, during a difficult passage for the violin section, Kohlberg deliberately stopped playing, laid down his violin, took off his glasses and started cleaning them. Reiner looked on in astonishment, finally stopped the orchestra and cried out, "What are you doing, Kohlberg?"—to which Kohlberg replied quietly, "I had a spot of dust on my lens, and with it there, I thought I might miss your beat!" For a moment Reiner did not know whether to respond with fury—or a smile, and fortunately for all, he chose the smile. I do believe that almost anyone else would have been thrown out of the orchestra immediately.

Photographed in Pittsburgh, 1947.

Claudio Arrau

Long after most musicians have reached the age of contentment and decided to rest on hard-earned laurels, Claudio Arrau keeps on playing. At his eightieth birthday concert in 1983, to name one notable event, he led off with two of Beethoven's most challenging sonatas—the *Waldstein* and the *Appassionata*—either of which, alone, would be challenge enough for any rational musician half his age. Yet the evidence exists, in a splendid videotape of the event: the old master charming a capacity Lincoln Center audience with the sweep and the majesty of his playing.

At the age of eight, already a musical hero in his native Chile, Arrau was sent by the Chilean government to study in Berlin. By 1914, he was already a touring virtuoso racking up concert dates in Germany and Scandinavia. He even studied composition, with a teacher none other than the young Kurt Weill. By 1921, still a teenager but with world renown already his, he returned to his native Chile, toured the Americas in triumph, and then returned for a time to a European base, performing such projects as a series of Bach concerts encompassing all the master's keyboard works, another series for Mozart, and, eventually and inevitably, the full cycle of the Beethoven "32." In 1941 he settled in New York.

Somewhat austere in manner, Arrau conceals a generous, giving nature. This comes out in his eagerness to teach, but it comes out as well in his playing. Like Schnabel before him, Arrau is most at home in big music—the classic repertory of sonatas and concertos. The bigness of his own musical outlook matches these grand structures, and fills them with warmth.

The morning I photographed Claudio Arrau, he had been held up getting to Pittsburgh and arrived at the rehearsal quite late.

At one point in the rehearsal, Reiner, never known as a pianist, casually sat down at the piano and started playing the Beethoven Fourth Piano Concerto, for which Arrau had been scheduled. It begins with an introduction for piano solo. Then the orchestra came in as one man, and we continued playing through the first movement while Reiner performed the piano part with remarkable skill, from memory. At the conclusion, Reiner received a standing ovation from the entire orchestra.

Photographed in Orange County, 1987.
Photographed in Pittsburgh, 1947.

Robert Casadesus

The Casadesus family has produced over three generations of distinguished French musicians. François founded the famous Academy at Fontainebleau, and his brother Henri was one of the first proponents of authentic early-music performance, with his famous New Society for Ancient Instruments. Their nephew Robert became in his day a beloved pianist, in solos or in duets with his wife Gaby; and *their* son, Jean, was on his way to a bright spot in the pianistic firmament when he was killed in an auto accident in Canada in 1972.

Robert's music-making was everything French: an eminent sensibility that sought out the symmetry, the logic in everything he played. He was at his incomparable best in Mozart, for which his playing defined above all the Age of Reason. Not for Casadesus, the Mozart of the Romantic era, with the same intensification as a Chopin or Brahms might merit.

The Casadeusus spirit also illuminated music of lesser stature as well. He could turn a witty if lightweight Saint-Saëns concerto into a genial discourse. But his Mozart—that remains truly memorable; there the spirit of Robert Casadesus was truly at home.

Photographed in Pittsburgh, 1946.

Bruno Walter

There used to be a sort of easy duality of music-lovers' jargon: Toscanini, the firebrand vs. the gentler, more benevolent Bruno Walter. Records and tapes of rehearsals emphasized the differences: Toscanini hurling imprecations at his hapless musicians, Walter consoling them gently.

Fortunately, these distinctions are never so easy in real life. The sweet-tempered Bruno Walter may have earned the love of his players, but that softness of disposition hardly spilled over into his actual music making. There is a passionate, surging side to his musicianship that belied his gentle exterior. Anyone who hears, for example, his legendary Vienna recording of the first act of Richard Wagner's *Die Walküre,* with Lotte Lehmann and Lauritz Melchior, will marvel at the power of Walter's orchestra.

His early association with Gustav Mahler made Walter the logical choice to spearhead the long-overdue restoration of Mahler's symphonic legacy. That, clearly, was no task for a mild-mannered conductor. However, hearing Walter's command over the last movement of the Mahler Ninth, for example, that white-hot strand of endless melody that seems to draw into itself the very breathing of its audience, you hear the work of a supreme master of emotional flow. The wonder is that he communicated the essence of this music to every musician who played under his probing, loving baton.

Photographed in Los Angeles, 1949.

Jascha Heifetz

Jascha Heifetz was a quiet man, with a seemingly impassive countenance. He spoke little, granted few interviews. Living in Los Angeles, he was eventually lured into the movie studios—why not, since Jascha Heifetz was in his day a household name among musicians, matched only by Horowitz and Toscanini? But in that movie—*They Shall Have Music*, with Heifetz sharing top billing with the Dead End Kids—all one could glean of the great violinist was the image of a man profoundly uncomfortable in his new role.

Heifetz seemed at home, in fact, only with his violin. In a sense, he was a throwback to a less complex time in music, when sheer virtuosity and the excitement it generated was reason enough for a soloist to have a successful career. Heifetz lived and performed long enough to see the musical world change its outlook.

Musical scholars late in his lifetime began to note the absence of a pure "Bach style" or a "Mozart style" in Heifetz's playing. There was a "Heifetz" style in everything he did, and that was enough to thrill listeners—and send other violinists into dark despair. There was a grand sweep in the Heifetz style that nobody could touch.

It's true that there will never be another Heifetz, but that's a little like saying that there will never be another Taj Mahal. One was enough.

Brooks Smith, a friend of mine and accompanist to Jascha Heifetz, once called to ask if I would turn pages for him while he and Mr. Heifetz recorded the Beethoven Kreutzer Sonata. I said I would be happy to on the condition that I be allowed to take pictures during the session. That request apparently caused several conferences, but Brooks finally called back and said that Mr. Heifetz had agreed. During the recording session, Mr. Heifetz fortunately was in a charming, relaxed mood and I took many pictures of him—smiling—and playing the piano as well as the violin.

A few days after the session, Brooks called and said they had to do some retakes and would I be available again. At that point I had my pictures and had some very pressing business matters, so I suggested a violinist friend who would be honored to assist at the session. I subsequently got a frantic call from Brooks to please come immediately to the session and help out, which I did. It turned out that Mr. Heifetz, king of violinists, had noticed a rash on the left side of my friend's jaw (which proclaimed him a violinist) and for no other reason had immediately ordered him to leave the studio!

Photographed in Los Angeles, 1957.

Arturo Toscanini

He was, to be sure, a genius: a man transfixed by a vision, doomed to endless torture as that vision remained ever so slightly out of reach. No aggregation of orchestral musicians could have given Arturo Toscanini the quality of performance he dreamed of; no amount of deep study on Toscanini's own part could have revealed every last secret in the music he played. One of the more aching Toscanini stories concerned a Mozart performance that he regarded as a failure. He rushed to his dressing room, and confronted his image in a mirror. "Old man!" he shrieked.

By the standards of the outside world, there weren't many such failures. Even after the public-relations hype, which the broadcasters and the record manufacturers piled up around Toscanini in his last years, is cleared away, we are confronted with the man who raised the standards of worldwide orchestral performance higher than anyone before him, who cut through the self-indulgent image-making of some of his colleagues by refusing to regard performing personality above the integrity of the composer's own score.

It is not true that Toscanini invented the notion of "performing the music exactly as written." That would be impossible, since the inevitable gap between the printed page and the live performance exists to be filled in with the personality of the performer. But Toscanini's personal magic did stand apart from that of many other conductors of his day, when the "what" of music often took second place to the "how."

The records don't fill in the Toscanini picture; he was in his sixties when he recorded his first symphony. What he must have accomplished, at the Met in, say, 1915, we can only guess. It must have been wonderful, though!

I photographed Toscanini in Pasadena when he was on tour with the NBC orchestra. His manager told me I could photograph the maestro during rehearsal, but to be far enough back in the auditorium so that I would not be seen.

I sat about halfway back, but even so the maestro's sharp ears would catch the click of my camera shutter and his head would spin around so that I would have to duck behind the seat each time. The picture I chose is interesting because it shows his extreme nearsightedness. It has been said that because of this problem he felt it necessary to memorize all his scores. His young conducting admirers chose to copy this approach and it subsequently became standard procedure for all future conductors, regardless if they were myopic or not.

Photographed in Pasadena, 1949.

Joseph Szigeti

In an age of spellbinding virtuoso violinists, one man stood apart. The playing of Joseph Szigeti may have lacked the seduction of the Heifetz tone; he never cultivated the golden vibrato of Mischa Elman. Yet he was one of those special performers who proudly wore the epithet of "musician's musician." You always came away from a Szigeti performance far more aware of the music than the way it was played.

You could guess Szigeti's own musical probity from the musicians he chose as collaborators: Artur Schnabel, with whom he gave legendary performances of Beethoven Violin Sonatas (never, alas, recorded) and especially his countryman Bela Bartok. In concerts at Carnegie Hall and at the Library of Congress in Washington these two expatriate Hungarians laid bare the intensity, the sheer creative fury of everything they played. Bartok dedicated some of his most important music to Szigeti; so did Prokofiev, Stravinsky and Bloch.

There is no better performance of anything on records than Szigeti's intense probing of the Bloch Violin Concerto, possibly that composer's masterpiece. But Szigeti, standing tall, motionless, totally wrapped in his music, could also turn on unexpected lights even in familiar repertory—in the Mendelssohn Concerto, which he recorded with Sir Thomas Beecham, or in the Bach Solo Sonatas, which he recorded with only Bach as collaborator.

Photographed in Los Angeles, 1950.

Igor Stravinsky

He was small in stature, but he cast a giant shadow. One could say of Igor Stravinsky that he belonged to that very small circle of musical innovators who had literally changed the direction of their art.

That happened, as every music student knows, in a theater in Paris on May 29, 1913, on the occasion of the premiere of Stravinsky's ballet *Le Sacre du Printemps*. Bad enough, for the astounded audience that night, that Vaclav Nijinsky's choreography employed strange pagan dance steps far removed from the traditional balletic language; Stravinsky's music, with its unheard-of combinations of instruments, its violence of rhythms and sounds caused in turn, a violence of reaction. As the music made the rounds of the orchestra halls in the early 1920s, each audience, each set of critics, tried to outdo the last in the fervor of their anger. The critics didn't survive, however; the music did.

Stravinsky spent the rest of his life changing styles and exciting audiences. From the violent rhythms of *Le Sacre* he turned to a cool, cerebral neoclassicism, composing an elephants' ballet for the Ringling Brothers, collaborating with Walt Disney on *Fantasia* with *Le Sacre* again, cut down to half its length, and in his last works espousing the twelve-tone methods of his one-time arch rival, Arnold Schönberg. His last years were spent in Beverly Hills, where he gave the world a steady stream of new work and an abrasive stream of critical essays.

When Stravinsky came to San Francisco in the 1940s to conduct the orchestra in some of his compositions, he had not yet mastered the art of conducting an orchestra. Rehearsals quickly degenerated into near chaos as Stravinsky mumbled his requests into the thick towel he wore around his neck. Fortunately, his friend and collaborator Pierre Monteux was in town and quickly saved the day in his usual masterful way.

Photographed in in Los Angeles, 1952.

Mario Castelnuovo-Tedesco

Los Angeles in the 1930s and 1940s was the most cosmopolitan musical capital anywhere in the world. Thanks to the proscriptive policies of Hitler and Mussolini, many of the greatest names in the arts were obliged to leave their homeland. Los Angeles lured many of them, not only with its benign climate, but also because of the movies. Many studio executives were, after all, themselves refugees; composers and writers flocked to their offices, in hopes that the movies would become the great artistic medium of the 20th century. Up against the realities—that the studios were really out for maximum attendance and maximum take—many of the world's finest artists found disillusionment.

Mario Castelnuovo-Tedesco arrived in Los Angeles in 1939. In his native Italy he had composed a phenomenal amount of music: operas, symphonies, chamber works—charming, fluent pieces, not much tinged by the new-music currents of the time. He continued in that vein in his new world, with a Guitar Concerto for Andrés Segovia that became exceptionally popular. He also possessed the magic formula for films, and of the twenty or so movies he scored, at least one—René Clair's *And Then There Were None*—still shows up in revival houses and on videotape.

In 1947 the Los Angeles conductor and composer Nat Shilkret developed a plan to keep the refugee composers busy: a collaborative suite of orchestral pieces illustrating various episodes from the Book of Genesis. Igor Stravinsky and Arnold Schönberg contributed, their arch-rivalry subjugated for the day; so did Castelnuovo-Tedesco. As his subject, he chose "Noah and the Ark."

Photographed with Stravinsky in Los Angeles, 1955.

Sir Thomas Beecham

Thomas Beecham arrived with his name already famous; Beecham Pills, ran the advertisements in the best British periodicals, were "just the thing"—for anemia, principally, among other ailments they were reputed to correct. There was nothing anemic about the scion to the pill fortune, however, or about his music-making. Forsaking a life that could easily have been that of an indolent British gentlemen, he went furiously about the task of bettering his countrymen's taste in serious music, and broadening their horizons as well. He performed contemporary music, championing such little-honored composers in their time as Richard Strauss and Frederick Delius. He also played Mozart and Haydn symphonies with an interpretive honesty rare among conductors at the turn of the century, avoiding the over-romanticization others tended to visit upon those noble composers.

A Beecham concert was always an adventure, for the players and for the audience as well. He would, upon the slightest whim, wheel about on the podium to chat with the audience—about the music, about proper behavior, about whatever was on his busy, darting mind. Possessed of a scathing wit, he would hurl his barbs at errant performers and drive many of them to despair. But he also earned their respect; beneath that prickly exterior there lurked a musicianly soul.

His art lives on in recordings, not only the majestic Handel and Mozart but also the tidbits—"lollipops," he liked to call them—that brightened up his programming: a dance from some forgotten ballet, a lighter-than-air overture. According to Sir Thomas; there was no small music, only small performers. He was one of the big ones.

Photographed in San Francisco, 1955.

Otto Klemperer

In his long and troubled life, Otto Klemperer had what might be described as three separate careers. In the vigorous artistic ferment of 1920s Berlin he was a staunch activist; in concerts, and at his own Kroll Opera—a sort of experimental wing of the Berlin State Opera, given over to new scores and iconoclastic staging—he conducted premieres of a huge amount of new music, some of it still in the repertory. Then, at the rise of Nazi power, Klemperer joined the mass exodus of some of Germany's finest artists, and made his way to Los Angeles.

There, from 1933 to 1939, he led the Los Angeles Philharmonic, giving that city its first hearings of Mahler symphonies and other out-of-the-way fare. In 1939, however, a massive stroke left him partially paralyzed and seemed to spell the end of his career.

Not so, however; after several years of painful recovery he again took up the baton. Walter Legge, artistic director of EMI records in London (known as Angel records in their American release) guided Klemperer to his third career. His enormous body bent and partially crippled but his mind still fresh and creative, Klemperer inscribed virtually the totality of the classic repertory on records: Beethoven symphonies, Mozart operas, Brahms, Mahler. When he could, he continued to tour and appear as guest conductor. That he could barely control a clear downbeat seemed not to matter; those privileged to play under him followed the great spirit of the man.

Otto Klemperer was a giant of a man, who never had to use a podium when conducting. His musical and physical presence was overwhelming.

He once asked me to play a chamber music concert consisting of the Bach Brandenburg Concertos at USC. I had asked and been given his permission to photograph him during rehearsal. This was after he had suffered a stroke which had partially paralyzed his body and face.

During rehearsal, I laid down my cello, picked up my camera and knelt at his feet to get an interesting angle. At this point he slowly raised his huge left foot, scowling at me all the while, and made as if he were going to smash me and my camera. Then his face broke into a strange smile and he waved me to continue on, as if it were a great joke.

Photographed in Los Angeles, 1955.

Pablo Casals

When he was born in 1876, the world had not yet heard Brahms' First Symphony; when he died, ninety-seven years later, electronic music was all the rage. For most of that century, the small, shy man from Catalonia had been a dominant figure on the musical landscape—as a cellist ("the greatest ever to draw a bow," a colleague once said), a conductor, a teacher and also, for a time, a recluse from all of that activity, a noble, single-minded protester against the immorality visited upon his Spain.

Casals was, in a sense, a kind of throwback. In his book of conversations, he already expressed doubts about the future of music, based on the "modernism" of composers we now accept as classics—Debussy, for one. No young cellist today would allow himself the liberties with tempo and dynamics that abound in the Casals recordings of the Bach Suites for solo cello.

For this very reason, perhaps, Casals remains in a class by himself. He defined his time among us simply, as a quest for beauty; what authority nowadays, however profound his knowledge of authentic performance practice, can dispute Casals' ideals? "Color . . . variety! . . ." on tapes of his master classes, we hear him exhort his students, over and over, to honor those timeless musical virtues. With his cello, on the podium, or simply in his teacher's chair, he gave his life to a kind of music-making that was to sing its heart out. That kind of passion can never become old-fashioned.

As a cellist, I had always admired Pablo Casals. In 1956, my wife and I planned a trip to Europe, and Casals was living in Prades, a French village close to the Spanish border. A friend and colleague, Milton Thomas, had written to him a month before, saying that I would like to meet him.

I tried telephoning him when we were in Europe, but learned he had no telephone. So one day we took a chance, drove to Prades and just knocked on his door. Even though I was a complete stranger with no appointment, he welcomed us with open arms and we had a cordial conversation, during which he asked if I would like him to play for us. I was overwhelmed, and of course said yes. He then took out his cello and asked me what I would like him to play. I mentioned the First Suite for solo cello by Bach, whereupon he played the entire suite—all six movements—with all the repeats, as if in concert performance.

Photographed in Prades, France, 1956.

Mstislav Rostropovich

What drives Mstislav Rostropovich? Nobody knows for sure; but behind his cello—residing at a rakish angle on its unusually long bent spike—or on the podium of his "own" Washington National Symphony, there is a feverish pitch in his music-making. He came to conducting only after he had conquered his cello; now he is completely at ease in both worlds. Sometimes the result of his volatility shows up as a performance somewhat larger than the music at hand; always the result is a great excitement. Many composers have written for him: Shostakovich and Prokofiev in his native land, Benjamin Britten, among others, in the West.

The tides of history have caught up with Rostropovich. His fierce championing of other outspoken Soviet dissidents—Alexander Solzhenitsin, most notably—cost him his citizenship and his rights to perform in his native land. America, his adopted land, has honored him well enough to make amends, but the ultimate victory came late in 1989, when his proscription shattered in the warm wave of *glasnost*. He returned a hero; he deserved no less.

Taken backstage at the old Philharmonic Auditorium during his first tour of the United States.

Photographed in Los Angeles, 1956.

William Steinberg

William Steinberg, a conductor of solid achievement in his native Germany pre-Hitler, was forced out of his post as head of the Frankfurt Opera. Arriving eventually in America, his rising star led him successively to the podiums of the Buffalo Philharmonic, the Pittsburgh Symphony and the Boston Symphony. Along the way, furthermore, he passed through Palestine, where he assisted Arturo Toscanini in founding the orchestra now known as the Israel Philharmonic.

William Steinberg's post-Hitler life consisted of a series of triumphs, bringing to each of his orchestral jobs the probity and serious artistic conscience of a man steeped in the classical repertory, but also responsive to the new music of his time. (In Frankfurt, after all, he had brought Alban Berg's *Wozzeck* into that city's operatic repertory.) A stolid, chunky man on the podium, with a bullet-shaped head and a tiny, meticulous but undemonstrative beat, he was never known as a showman, but always as an honest musician of impeccable taste.

Steinberg was never known for his matinee-idol features. After taking pictures of him in the Hollywood Bowl, I met him backstage and he told me his manager had suggested that he reduce the size of his nose by plastic surgery, to which he had responded, "Cut off my nose? They should cut off my head."

Photographed in Los Angeles, 1958.

Serge Koussevitzky

The world needs more like him: the conductor who has risen to the heights, who could easily have rested on his laurels and conducted concerts of easy, popular classics. Yet, he was a fierce fighter for new music from his early days in his native Russia to Paris and to Boston, where for nearly thirty years he single-handedly redefined the role of a symphony orchestra as the bastion of progressiveness in the arts.

In doing so he also created an instrument like no other: an orchestra with a tone as of the finest silk. It sometimes wasn't the proper fabric for wrapping the classics, but the sound of Koussevitzky's orchestra in, say, Debussy or Ravel, was like nothing else in the world.

An amazing number of works considered latter-day classics came to life first under Koussevitzky: Stravinsky's *Symphony of Psalms*, Bartok's Concerto for Orchestra, Prokofiev's Fifth Symphony. When the critics kicked up their heels over some controversial work, Koussevitzky would reschedule it for a second hearing that season. He ran the Boston Symphony with an iron hand, and seemed to run the rest of Boston's culture—and westward, to the Tanglewood Music Festival—no less autocratically.

In thirty years in Boston he mastered perhaps a dozen English words, and those badly. He needed no more; the world learned to come to him.

While I was taking pictures of Koussevitsky and Rubinstein at the Hollywood Bowl, a heated argument erupted between them. They started shouting in Russian which fortunately I understood. Rubinstein was complaining that Koussevitsky was taking the tempo much too slow, that it was killing him, to which Koussevitsky responded with but one word, "Khoroshow [Good!]."

Photographed in Los Angeles, 1957.

Vladimir Horowitz

Skilled as Vladimir Horowitz surely was in the ways of the piano—he was no less adept in an even more impressive art: the making of living legends.

The legend arrived with the pianist, in fact—on January 12, 1928, when the twenty-four-year-old Russian firebrand chanced to make his New York debut alongside that of another equally touted newcomer, Sir Thomas Beecham. The stories, verified or otherwise, are still around about that night, with each newcomer out to run circles around the other, with Tchaikovsky's First Piano Concerto as the battleground.

The Horowitz career, right up to his death in 1989, continued to make marvelous copy: his astonishing technique, his uses of that technique in show-off piano tidbits of no recognizable value, his frequent "retirements" from concert life, his wonderfully orchestrated returns, the famous return to Moscow in 1986 after sixty years absence, the ardent TV documentation of virtually his every move—alas, too late in the long span of his lifetime to represent much of the qualities that had once made his name a beacon of virtuosity and intimidation.

Simply stated, Horowitz played too long; in those last concerts you had to listen through a time warp: the figure on stage in the 1980s, the memory of the playing in the 1950s. That way, it wasn't hard to imagine the breadth, the might, of the Horowitz phenomenon.

Photographed in Los Angeles, 1958.

Pierre Monteux

No single episode in the annals of musical history has been more profusely documented than the goings-on in Paris at the Théâtre des Champs-Élysées on the night of May 29, 1913. The conductor, on that night of the world premiere (and attendant riot) of Igor Stravinsky's *Le Sacre du Printemps* was the thirty-eight-year-old Pierre Monteux, principal conductor of Serge Diaghilev's Ballets Russes and, thus, heir to a vast repertory of major new scores that Diaghilev and his company were introducing with astonishing regularity in those heady pre-war years.

But Monteux was destined for greater things than life in a ballet pit. The genial, twinkling man—the twinkle masking a demonic sense of inner purpose—moved on to command the Boston Symphony in 1919, holding firm even through a disastrous orchestral strike. His growing career brought him to the Metropolitan Opera, to San Francisco—where he led that city's orchestra to glory for seventeen years starting in 1936—and to engagements around the world. Beloved by his musicians, he also found time to lead classes for the training of young conductors, in a summer institute he founded in Hancock, Maine.

The Stravinsky shocker of 1913 remained in Monteux's baggage; his later performances of *Le Sacre* had a violent drive coupled with an almost classic clarity that set them apart from all other performances. But Monteux's musical version was, like his own lovable, waddling figure, remarkably broad; there are Beethoven and Brahms recordings under him, direct and spaciously planned, not at all what you'd expect from the characteristic French approach to the classics.

I had the pleasure of working under Pierre Monteux for six years in the San Francisco Symphony. He was a very great conductor and was admired and respected by all whose lives he touched.

Photographed in Los Angeles, 1958.

Leon Fleisher

At age six, Leon Fleisher gave his first public concert—in his native San Francisco—and already there was a prodigy clearly in the making. Studies in the Bay Area with the famous Lev Shorr led to the chance to work with the formidable, legendary Artur Schnabel, in Italy and later in New York. Of all the Schnabel students, Leon Fleisher seemed the most qualified to take on the master's special mantle. He was serious, dedicated, obsessed with the classics and with no-frills programming, as Schnabel always was. His early recordings—the Brahms Concertos with George Szell, and the Brahms "Handel" Variations, were connoisseur items from the day they appeared.

At the peak of Fleisher's career, disaster struck. A mysterious neurological affliction made it impossible for him to move the fingers of his right hand. The malady was later diagnosed as "carpal tunnel syndrome" and Fleisher was its most famous victim. He took up conducting, and has been leading orchestras with increasing frequency. He also applied himself to the limited repertory of piano music for the left hand alone, much of it composed for the Austrian virtuoso Paul Wittgenstein, who had lost his right arm in World War I.

Fleisher has also developed into an outstanding teacher, and is head of the piano faculty at the Peabody Conservatory. In addition, he is currently artistic director of the Tanglewood Music Festival.

Photographed in Los Angeles, 1958, 1990, 1977.

John Browning

John Browning, one of America's brightest and best, came under the tutelage of Rosina Lhevinne at the age of ten, when the great lady was conducting a master class in Browning's native Denver. Later the family moved to Los Angeles, where John studied with Lee Pattison; then to New York, Juilliard and, once again, Lhevinne. Along the way there was the prestigious Leventritt Award. That happened in 1955; Van Cliburn had won the same prize a year earlier.

For the slender, movie-star handsome Browning, the real breakthrough came in 1962, when he was chosen to introduce Samuel Barber's Piano Concerto, composed for the opening ceremonies at Manhattan's Lincoln Center. A smashing piece in the old-fashioned virtuosic manner, Barber's Concerto has served Browning well; by his own calculations, he performed it four hundred times in the twenty years following its premiere, while finding time for other projects—recording the five Piano Concertos of Prokofiev with the Boston Symphony, for example—as well.

Years ago my wife and I were in Paris and we were visited by our longtime friend, John Browning. There was a break in the Brussels piano competition and John had come to Paris for a day or two to relax. He told us he thought he was doing quite well, but there was a young kid whose piano playing scared the hell out of him—a then-unknown by the name of Vladimir Ashkenazy. His fears proved to be well founded when Ashkenazy won first prize and John second. However, the rigors of the competition took their toll on Ashkenazy and he was unable to accept one of the prizes, a tour of the Soviet Union. John then stepped in and had a triumphant success in his first Soviet tour.

Photographed in Los Angeles, 1986, 1986, 1955.

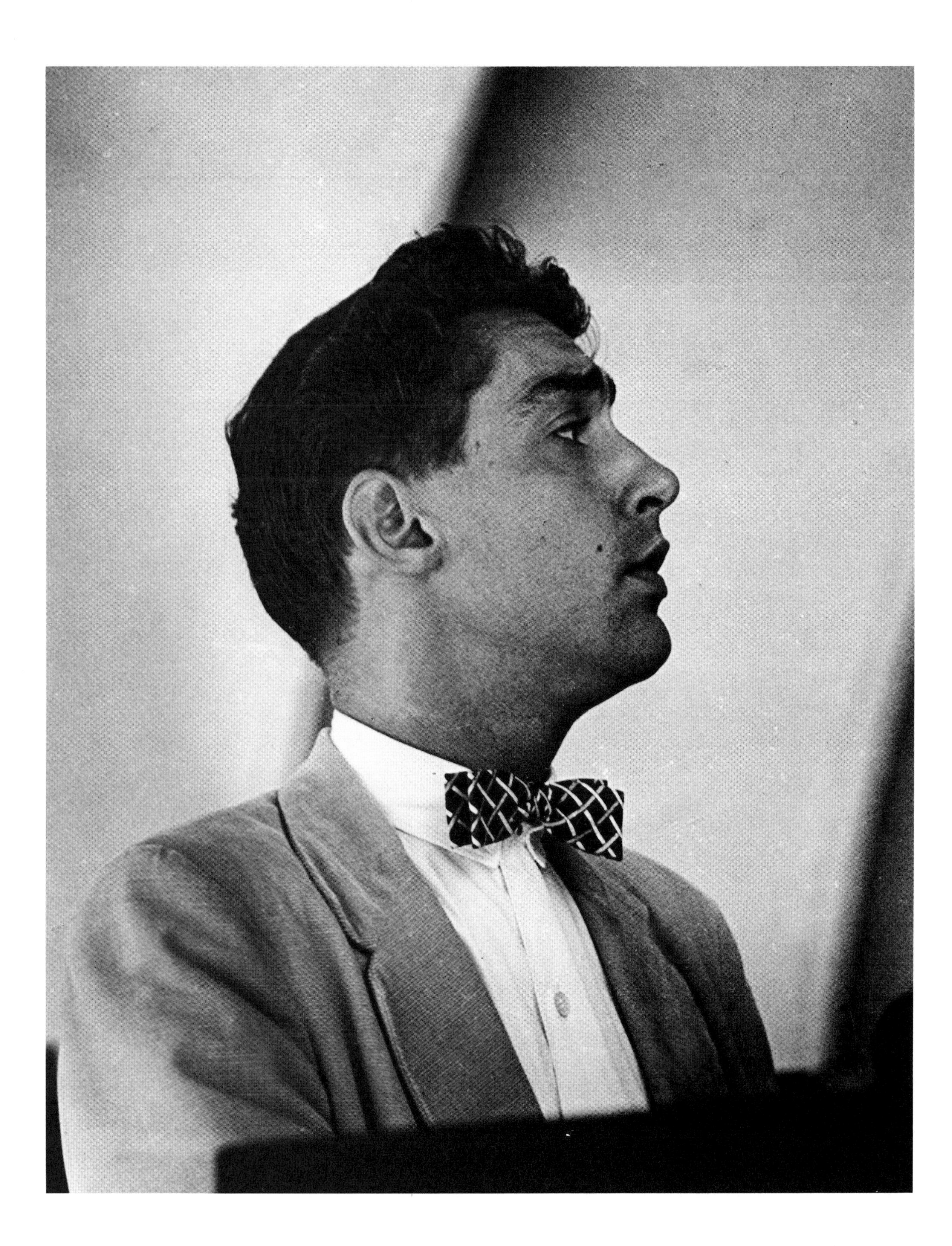

Isaac Stern

Isaac Stern is a sublimely talented violinist, adept in the standard repertory and in challenging new works as well. He is also the paradigm of a caring citizen of the world. He came out from behind his violin to spearhead the rescue of Carnegie Hall from the wreckers' ball; lead a later drive to rebuild and restore the hall when the walls had begun to crumble on their own. He speaks out often on behalf of human rights.

Not merely a stand-offish virtuoso, he often joins forces with other colleagues and students in chamber music; his trio recordings with Eugene Istomin and the late Leonard Rose are some of the best chamber performances recorded. He has helped other young musicians—notably Pinchas Zukerman and Itzak Perlman—early in their careers.

A musician of Stern's stature could be forgiven for simply resting on his laurels. The marvel of Stern—beyond the incidental fact that he happens to play the violin as well as, if not better than, any musician alive—is that he has harnessed that fame for the betterment of the entire cultural world.

At one time I had gone backstage to congratulate Isaac Stern on a particularly brilliant performance. Just ahead of me in the waiting line was an elderly woman who in a quavering voice said, "Mr. Stern, when you played tonight, God was standing next to you." Isaac quickly looked to his right and left and said, "That's funny, I didn't notice."

Photographed at the Hollywood Bowl, 1958.

Arthur Rubinstein

Nobody could have invented Arthur Rubinstein—nobody, that is, but himself, and it was a task that kept him happily busy for ninety-five years. Forget about the majesty of his accomplishments at the keyboard for a moment; just the outlines of the life he led, the passion for sampling everything in our civilization that makes it, well, civilized, confirm his stature as the archetypal Personage of the Arts. Even if those epicurean accountings of great dining and lovemaking and contacts with other denizens of the Olympian slopes were only half true, they would still establish the Rubinstein aura as a source of awe and affection.

The greatness of Rubinstein is that his music stands, not apart from his personal life (as it might in the case of, say, a Heifetz) but as its culmination. The aristocratic mind that shapes those melting phrases in the Nocturnes of Chopin is the logical extension of the mind well fed at the host's table, well nourished as well by the conversational games at countless convivial evenings.

Aristocratic: that, above all, is the nature of the Rubinstein artistry. And when there is that moment—in unexpected places, in a Villa-Lobos piece for children, or in the unfolding of sheer love in a quiet, rippling Schumann Arabesque—there is nothing to do but to stand aside in delight at the notion that one mere mortal can create so much beauty in so little time.

Photographed in Los Angeles, 1958.

Van Cliburn

Van Cliburn was, and is, an authentic American-style hero. Tall, curly-haired and dimpled; it worked for Charles A. Lindbergh in Paris in 1927 and it worked for Cliburn at the First Tchaikovsky Competition in Moscow in 1958. Both heroes received ticker-tape parades for their accomplishment.

Naysayers would have you believe that any American could have won that Moscow competition, that it made political sense for that kind of gesture. Nonsense; Cliburn, with the much-respected Leventritt Award under his belt already, was a young American pianist clearly bound for the high echelons. The music-making that followed the Moscow triumph bore out Cliburn's impeccable credentials; the records remain to make it clear that Van Cliburn, at one time, was beyond question our greatest young pianist.

We'll probably never know what prompted Cliburn to step away from the footlights in the late 1970s. In any case, there was nothing but silence from Cliburn's piano for nearly a decade. And when he made his reentry, at the opening of a new concert hall in Dallas in the fall of 1989, the notices were more respectful than effusive.

Never let it be said, however, that the tall Texan does not serve his art these days. He does so with his personal involvement in the quadrennial Van Cliburn Piano Competition in his native Fort Worth. The competition personifies the magic and heartbreak of the whole struggle toward success in music. For that very reason, it belongs with the name of Van Cliburn.

Photographed in Los Angeles, 1959.

Kirill Kondrashin

We first learned of Kirill Kondrashin in America during the glory days of Van Cliburn's great celebration; it was Kondrashin who had conducted the orchestra in Moscow that had supported Cliburn's playing in the Tchaikovsky Competition of 1958. With open-hearted generosity, Cliburn shared that triumph, and when he repeated his prize-winning performances in America later that same year, Kondrashin was again on the podium—the first Soviet conductor to appear in the U.S.

Kondrashin was already highly regarded in his native U.S.S.R. by then, and his functioning as a "musical ambassador" to the West did him no harm. He did stir up a more Soviet brand of controversy with the premiere performance of the Thirteenth Symphony of Shostakovich, with its inflammatory choral texts by Yvtushenko that were said to displease Khruschev most gravely.

Kondrashin's last years were spent in a lively flirtation with the West, including appearances at that capitalist bastion, the Hollywood Bowl. As a direct link with the great Russian romantic style, he enjoyed a deserved success worldwide. At the time of his death, in 1981, he had been appointed permanent conductor of the great Amsterdam Concertgebouw Orchestra; he collapsed and died immediately after a concert there.

Photographed in Los Angeles, 1959.

Aaron Copland

If a single figure can stand for the integrity of America's serious musical tradition, let Aaron Copland be that figure. Think of our new-music scene before Copland in the 1920s: a few solitary experimenters like Ives and Cowell, but nothing to find its way into the repertory of the major music-makers. It was Copland's generation, nurtured for a time in Paris and Berlin, but eventually at home back in its native land, that first created music of symphonic substance, music that partook of the most progressive trends of its time, music that also reflected the particulars of its own country.

Copland's music embraced it all: the early, wildly dissonant pieces from Paris, the flirtation with jazz in the Piano Concerto, the great translations of Americana into ballet scores like *Rodeo* and *Billy the Kid*, a time in Hollywood, a touch of opera, a later synthesis of many of these currents in the big mature works—in the radiance of *Appalachian Spring* and the tough, craggy *Piano Fantasy* and the *Connotations*.

It has been a long good musical journey, for this Brooklyn-born hero-artist who never lost the accent of his hometown, in his music or his speech. Heaven only knows the course of American music without Copland to fling wide the doors. Something, surely, would be missing.

Photographed in Aspen, 1960.

Rosina Lhevinne

She lived nearly a century; she died, at ninety-six, beloved the world over as musician and teacher. Rosina Bessie was already an acclaimed and promising young artist in her native Kiev when, at nineteen, she married the Russian virtuoso Josef Lhevinne, six years her senior and already clearly destined for top honors. The Lhevinnes emigrated to the U.S. after World War I where both Josef's solo career and the duo piano team with Rosina flourished until Josef's death in 1944.

Rosina, the great heart, did not stop. At the age of eighty-one, she played her first solo recital in America. There are records to attest to her loving, if old-fashioned, way of playing Mozart. Her greatest fame, however, was as a teacher, most of all as the head of the piano department at the Juilliard School. There the most famous of her pupils arrived in the early 1950s, a gangling, raw-talented Texas lad named Van Cliburn. Rosina sensed the gold in that great Cliburn spirit, mined and refined it with a perfectionist's loving touch. To Cliburn's great credit, he made it clear after his Moscow triumph that Rosina Lhevinne's heart and mind had shown him the way.

Her wisdom persists. "If you aspire to a career in music," she once said, "you have only to ask yourself this. Is music so essential to your artistic and spiritual nourishment that it simply *has* to be your life's work? If your answer is yes, you will eventually find a place."

Photographed with Brooks Smith in Aspen, 1960.

Ernst Toch

By the time Ernst Toch was obliged to leave his native Austria, he was widely known as a highly prolific and proficient composer, with three operas to his credit, eleven string quartets, a vast amount of orchestral and piano music. He had already moved from Vienna to Berlin; after Hitler's rise he lived for a time in Paris and London, stopped off in New York, and settled in Hollywood in 1936.

Among Los Angeles' European refugee contingent, Toch was one of the most successful. His relatively conservative, approachable style accorded well with the needs of the studios, and his movie triumphs include several anti-Nazi films (*None Shall Escape*, *Address Unknown*) along with such lighter fare as Bob Hope's *The Ghost Breakers*.

He continued a veritable fountainhead of music until his death, in 1964, although it is likely that history will winnow out a few works from among the many that deserve survival. Among these will surely be the *Pinocchio Overture*, a long-standing fixture at Pops concerts, and a truly remarkable choral work, his *Geographical Fugue*. This is a piece for speaking and singing chorus, made up entirely of a constant byplay among world names that Toch found especially appealing (Bolivia's Lake Titicaca, for one).

His Third Symphony (1956) won a Pulitzer Prize, and this honor undoubtedly led to a long-overdue recognition by the Austrian government. That gesture, in 1963, was too late; Toch died the next year.

Little known was the fact that Ernst Toch was an outstanding pianist. I had the privilege of premiering with him and his very fine piano quintet.

Photographed in Los Angeles, 1964.

David Oistrakh

Before World War II, the worldwide violinistic scene had already come under Russian conquest, thanks to the likes of Mischa Elman, Jascha Heifetz, and Nathan Milstein. In the last days of peace, word had crossed the Atlantic of a new challenger to those ranks, David Oistrakh, who at twenty-nine had carried off first prize in the 1937 Brussels Competition—in the days when a big competition win could really launch a career.

By the time Oistrakh made it to these shores, in 1955, his fame had already been established through recordings, and through the knowledge that the greatest composers of his country, Prokofiev and Shostakovich, had entrusted major works to the lush, singing tone of his inspired musicianship. By the time of his death, in 1974, Oistrakh had single-handedly restored the phenomenon of the romantic violinist to its pinnacle, at a time when that kind of larger-than-life playing had, everyone believed, begun to go out of style.

Even his son Igor, whom he taught—King David passing the torch to Prince Igor—grew into a different kind of violinist, more classically minded, less flamboyant. Stolid and undemonstrative on the stage, David Oistrakh more than compensated for his lack of visual drama by the intensity of his playing. He might have been the last of his breed, but there are the records—a glowing legacy—to signalize the scope of his accomplishment.

Taken in Vienna on Oistrackh's first tour outside of Russia with the Leningrad Orchestra and conductor Mravinsky.

Photographed in Vienna, 1956.
Photographed in Los Angeles, 1965.

Gregor Piatigorsky

Photographed in Los Angeles, 1976.

Leonard Bernstein

Our image of Leonard Bernstein remains fixed on that November day in 1943 when the smiling young conductor passed upward to instant and lasting celebrity, standing in for an ailing Bruno Walter to lead the New York Philharmonic on its weekly live broadcast concert. He didn't, at that moment, just come out of nowhere; he was the Philharmonic's assistant conductor, and stepping in for ailing top conductors was part of his job. Still, it hadn't happened before quite that way, to a young man barely twenty-five, American born and trained.

Would Bernstein have moved onward and upward as he did, without that lucky push? Of course he would; it might have taken a bit longer, however. Not much; in the year after that Philharmonic date he had produced a symphony (*Jeremiah*), a revolutionary jazz ballet (*Fancy Free*), and a Broadway musical (*On the Town*). He was off and running, in other words, and hasn't stopped yet.

Now, as a senior citizen, he has conquered the world many times over. The flamboyance of his podium manner has somewhat subsided, leaving behind the solid substance of a distinguished classical interpreter. Above all, Bernstein towers above the musical world as an enabling symbol, a message from his own experience that it is possible to hope for a serious musical career even if you're (1) American and (2) young.

He is one of the few authentic musical figures of whom it can be truthfully said: he left his world a different place from the one he first entered.

Mr. Bernstein was conducting at the Hollywood Bowl and I had heard of his podium gyrations. I fortunately caught him in one of them, and call it "Air Borne Maestro."

Photographed in Los Angeles, 1985.

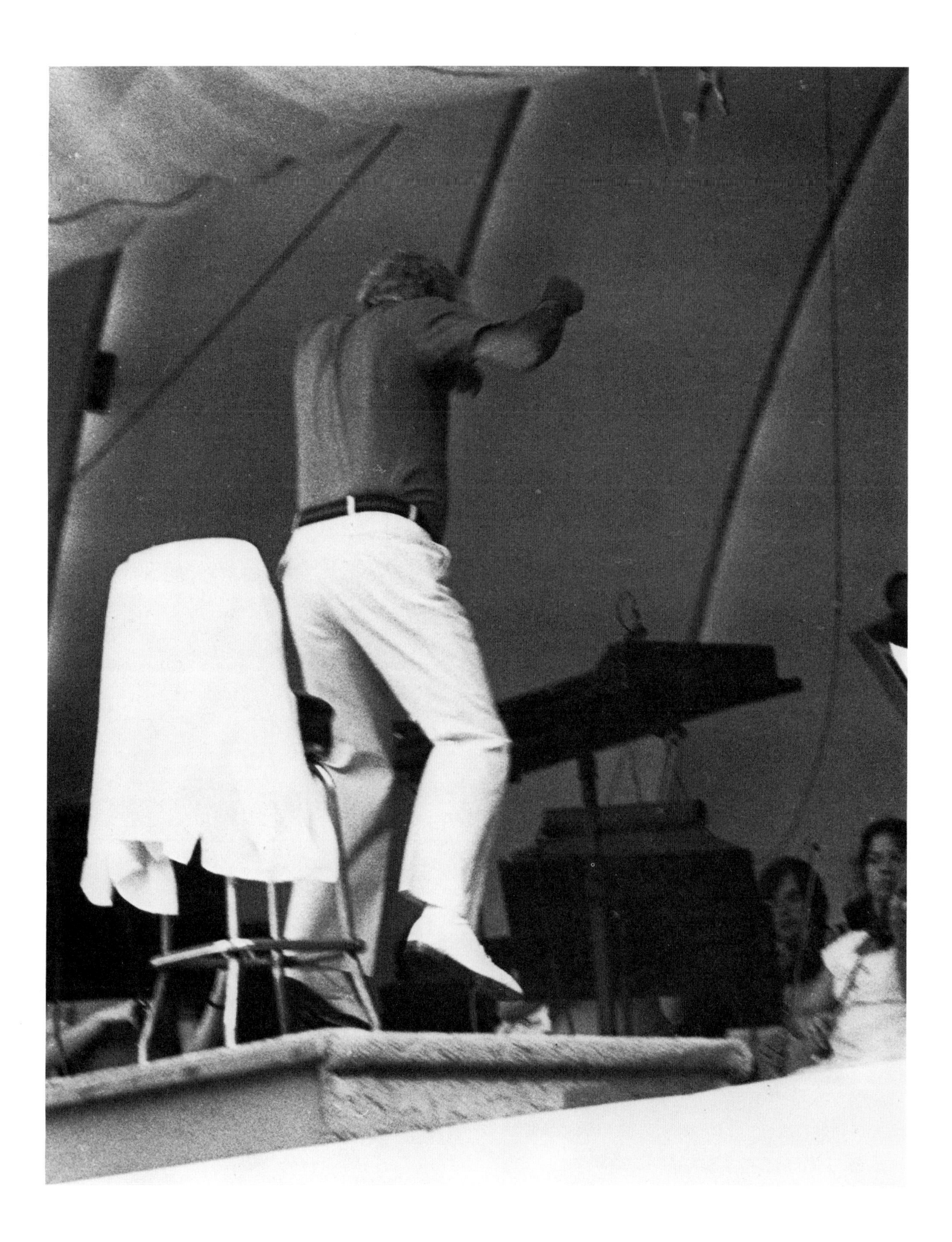

Vladimir Ashkenazy

Of all the greatly gifted musicians who came to prominence in the Soviet Union in the years following World War II, none has taken on more of a genuine world view than Vladimir Ashkenazy. Born in Gorky in 1937, son of two professional pianists, the young man showed exceptional promise from the beginning. When, in fact, he won the auspicious Queen Elisabeth prize in Brussels in 1956, there were grumblings that—even at nineteen—Ashkenazy was too well established as a worldwide virtuoso to be allowed to compete!

Ashkenazy came to the U.S. in 1958. A distant relative in New York tells how, when the young pianist arrived, he had no inkling of the Ashkenazis that were his ancestors—the European "family" whose history goes back to the time of the Crusades, and paid an astonished visit to an ancient Ashkenazic cemetery in lower Manhattan. This discovery of his heritage may have influenced Ashkenazy's decision to leave the Soviet Union; his official home is in Iceland.

In the early 1980s, with a distinguished following as one of the world's greatest pianists, Ashkenazy determined to conquer yet more territory. He began to conduct, found that he was good at it, and is currently Principal Guest Conductor of the Cleveland Orchestra.

Ashkenazy has a way of commanding attention on the podium. Strangely, his best orchestral repertory doesn't overlap his strengths as a pianist: on the one hand, the early romantic piano repertory of Schumann and Chopin, on the other, the great late-romantic warhorses—Sibelius especially. With a fine sense of balance, he has so far maintained both careers, simultaneously and well.

Photographed in Pasadena, 1985, 1988.
Photographed in Los Angeles, 1985.

Horacio Gutierrez

He bounds onto the stage, his round face all boyish grin. Here is a big, outspoken musician, and a good one: Horacio Gutierrez, born in Cuba in 1948, a student both there and, later, in Los Angeles and New York. In 1970 he was a silver medalist in Moscow's Tchaikovsky Competition, and it's easy to guess, from his playing, the elements that made the strongest impression on the judges in Moscow.

He is, if anything, too phenomenally endowed. Like his older countryman Jorge Bolet, Gutierrez knows no such thing as a technical problem. A work like the Second Piano Concerto of Prokofiev, widely acknowledged as the most finger-threatening of all the Russian repertory, becomes for this young Cuban a walk-away. He may, in fact, be the best interpreter of Prokofiev's piano music now in circulation; a 1988 Los Angeles performance of the seldom-heard Ninth Piano Sonata had a Music Center crowd gasping with wonderment.

Concerning the tenderer side of the romantic repertory, Gutierrez may have some distance still to cover. Critics have found some of his playing metronomic, as if he was afraid to unleash all the power that is his to command. When he overcomes that reticence, Horacio Gutierrez may indeed become the pianist of his generation most worth the watching.

Photographed in Los Angeles, 1985.

Andrei Gavrilov

Andrei Gavrilov, born in Moscow in 1955, was taught by his mother, a graduate of Moscow Conservatory. At eighteen, he won the 1974 Tchaikovsky Competition, which launched him on an international career.

At twenty, Gavrilov made his London debut in Royal Festival Hall, where he was welcomed with impressive critical and public acclaim. In September 1978 Gavrilov made his debut in Germany as soloist with the Berlin Philharmonic; he then played a thirty-concert tour of West Germany. With the Leningrad Philharmonic Orchestra, he toured Western Europe. In the summer of 1979 he made his debut in Japan, where he played twelve concerts, and in 1985 he played a highly acclaimed debut recital in Carnegie Hall.

Gavrilov has had an extremely successful recording career which brought him several prestigious international awards. He has recorded Tchaikovsky's First and Rachmaninoff's Third Piano Concerto with Muti and the Philharmonia Orchestra, Prokoviev's First Piano Concerto with Rattle and the Philharmonia Orchestra, and Tchaikovsky Concerti Nos. 1 and 3 with the Berlin Philharmonic and Ashkenazy.

Photographed in Pasadena, 1985.

Carlos Montoya

The origins of the great, passionate art known as flamenco are shrouded in his history and in controversy. Undoubtedly it comes from the colorful region known as Andalusia, but from whom? Gypsies, who wander frequently through the area? Arabs, who once settled there? Ancient Hebraic tribes, whose own music bears some resemblance? Perhaps all three?

There is less controversy about flamenco's greatest exponent. Carlos Montoya was born in Madrid, and was already a skilled guitarist by the age of eight. His first performances were with dance groups; he toured for a time with the great dancer La Argentina. The market for solo players in that folk idiom was slim—and remained so until Montoya himself became famous. Gradually his fame expanded; he has toured the Americas, Japan, Vietnam.

A self-taught musician, who has thrived without the need of such intellectual encumbrances as the ability to read printed music, Montoya has become synonymous with the insinuating, darkly passionate language of flamenco. He has composed, modestly to be sure: his *Flamenco Suite* is in every hopeful young player's repertory.

It's always a beautiful sight on a stage: a man and his guitar forming a sort of visual unity. Even before he begins to play, Montoya on stage is a commanding presence.

Photographed in Los Angeles, 1985.

Pinchas Zukerman

Call him "Pinky"; everybody does. Pinchas Zukerman (born Tel Aviv, 1948) is part of that musical gang that hangs out around Carnegie Hall and Lincoln Center and is known as the "Kosher Nostra" despite the fact that one of its members is the Parsi Zubin Mehta—and despite the fact that the other members include two other violinists, Stern and Perlman. Why aren't these three fiddlers at each other's throats?

It's probably that all three are so far ahead of the pack that it no longer matters. Furthermore, Pinky the violinist is only part of Zukerman's story; there is also Pinky the conductor and Pinky the violist, both eminently successful in their careers.

Pinky the violinist began his musical life at the tender age of six, studying first at home with his father, later at the Tel Aviv Conservatory. There he was heard by Stern, and also by Pablo Casals, who saw to his coming to New York and to lessons with the legendary Ivan Galamian. In 1967 a Leventritt Competition first prize really launched his career, which has been in orbit ever since.

Conducting was for Zukerman something of a lark at first—with early engagements with the Boston Symphony, New York Philharmonic and the Philadelphia, a most prestigious beginning. In 1980 he took over the St. Paul Chamber Orchestra, one of the most adventurous small ensembles in the country, and guided its destiny for seven years with the imagination and intelligence that marks all the work of this remarkably versatile musician.

Photographed with Perlman in New York, 1985.
Photographed in New York, 1985.

Itzak Perlman

There are many who consider Itzak Perlman the greatest violinist in the world, and there are few who are willing to argue the point. In his short lifetime—he was born in Tel Aviv in 1945—Perlman has successfully overcome two major handicaps, and has moved on to hero status on both counts. First, he has been crippled since the age of four, with a brutal polio attack that left both legs paralyzed. Second, he was discovered and vigorously exploited by the arch-marketeer of upcoming talent, Ed Sullivan.

Perlman is, in fact, the most potent refutation one could find of the notion that too much public exposure can wreck the integrity of a career. Perlman, from the start of his major career, has beautifully orchestrated the showbiz side of his life. He has played jazz with Isaac Stern. He has hung out in the White House, especially in the Reagan years. Even if he were to lose all contact with his precious violin, he could thrive as a TV comic and serious commentator.

His service to music is no less varied and valuable. As the outstanding virtuoso of his time, he could get by very well on the standard concerto repertory—Mendelssohn, Brahms, Beethoven, Tchaikovsky. In addition, however, he loves to explore the music of his own century; his recordings of the Alban Berg and Igor Stravinsky Violin Concertos need defer to no new-music specialist.

He is, in a matter of speaking, the complete musician of our time. More than that, however, Itzhak Perlman is also the complete *mensch*. That's harder.

Photographed with Zukerman and Kalichstein in New York, 1985.
Photographed in New York, 1985.

Henryk Szeryng

It wasn't until relatively late in his career that America discovered the peerless violin artistry of Henryk Szeryng. Born in Poland in 1918, Szeryng enjoyed a huge success almost from the start of his professional career. It started on a January day in 1918, when as a youth of fifteen he took on the formidable Brahms Violin Concerto with the Warsaw Philharmonic. There was no stopping him after that.

Szeryng was an unusual musician, the product of a broad mixture of performance philosophies that might have confused a less brilliant mind. From early lessons at the St. Petersburg Conservatory, he learned the grand virtuosic tradition that had also produced such contemporary prodigies as Jascha Heifetz. In Berlin, still a teenager, he learned the more straightforward classical style of the legendary Carl Flesch. Then there was a Paris sojourn, composition lessons with the formidable Nadia Boulanger, and an immersion in the visionary, romantic violinistic style of Jacques Thibaud.

The marvel of Szeryng's own playing became his ability to create a synthesis of his own from this varied background. You hear it in his extraordinary recording of the Bach Unaccompanied Sonatas and Partitas, extensive, complex works that can easily become mere studies in note-spinning. In Szeryng's performances every note becomes an element in a powerful dramatic progression.

A solid, undemonstrative player on stage, Szeryng reached his audiences purely through that mix of intelligence and virtuosity that one rarely finds in performers on any instrument. His last years were spent in Mexico, which he adopted as a homeland, and which he served well by playing the music of its composers.

I was photographing Henryk Szeryng and his pianist Karl Reiner at a rehearsal in the Ambassador Auditorium. I noticed that Reiner was having trouble turning the pages in a difficult piano piece, so I offered my services in turning the pages. He and Szeryng accepted, and later said that I was the best page-turner they had ever had—let alone a photographer who also knew when to turn the pages.

Reiner, it turned out was the nephew of Fritz Reiner, so we had a good time reminiscing after the rehearsal.

Photographed in Pasadena, 1986.

Walter Klien

His name is pronounced "clean," and he has had to endure the wordplay that that news engenders. Actually, the epithet is fairly apt; Walter Klien belongs to that splendid group of European pianists, most of them Austrian (Alfred Brendel, Paul Badura-Skoda, Joerg Demus) who have restored to prominence the serious heart of the classic repertory. Klien first attracted attention through his recordings, again devoted to the more serious side of the repertory: no big-bang virtuoso stuff, but beautifully spacious, unhurried performances of Mozart in which, in the very best sense, the performer seems to disappear into the music.

Klien was born in Graz in 1928. In his twenties, he won first prize—twice!—in the Concorso Busoni, one of the few competitions that prize individuality over the usual machine-made performances. Apparently, and commendably, nonchalant toward the lure of the virtuoso's glamorous life, he spends considerable time as a chamber musician, notably with his great countryman, the violinist Wolfgang Schneiderhan.

Modest as the dimensions of his career may be, Klien must be reckoned, at very least, a highly talented pianist. You come away from his performance thinking about the music, rather than the way it was played. That can be a rewarding experience.

Photographed in Pasadena, 1986.

Anton Kuerti

In the world of advertising, the Marlboro Man is a well-built creature with a cigarette in one hand, his eye on the far horizons of some idealized Western landscape. Music has another kind of Marlboro Man. He spends his summers at the Marlboro Music Festival on a small campus in southern Vermont. He passes the time playing chamber music with his colleagues. On weekends there are small-scale, informal concerts. The whole spirit at Marlboro is a loving dedication to the quieter kinds of music: Mozart, chamber music, Bach, Schubert.

Rudolf Serkin, the great, ecstatic genius of the keyboard, is the governing spirit at Marlboro, and from his benevolent caretaking a generation of pianists has emerged that share his own passions. Serkin's son Peter was one of the first Marlboro products; in his wake there followed Murray Perahia, Richard Goode, Ruth Laredo . . . and Anton Kuerti.

Kuerti was actually born in Vienna, but emigrated to the U.S. at an early age. Before arriving at Serkin's doorstep (actually, at Serkin's master class at the Curtis Institute) he had worked with another legendary benevolence, the late Arthur Loesser at the Cleveland Institute. Later he would migrate to Canada, to become professor of piano at the University of Toronto, and to make an impressive recording of the complete Beethoven Sonatas at the behest of the Canadian branch of CBS records.

But it is the Marlboro Man in Kuerti that one first thinks of: the patient, warm-hearted, loving friend to the classics. Not many pianists can match the honest modesty of his style; cherish it.

Photographed in Pasadena, 1986.

Gary Karr

You've never heard anything like a family reunion of the Karr family. Young Gary (born in 1941) came by his calling honorably; his father was a double-bass player, so was his grandfather, so were two uncles and three cousins.

The bass is a noble instrument, quite literally the foundation on which the entire tone of a symphony orchestra rests. Yet a solo career on the double-bass: that's something else. There simply isn't very much to play. There are the trick pieces: minor Italian works by 19th-century bassists who liked to write hilarious duets for bass and piccolo. There are some chamber pieces—among them Schubert's beloved *Trout* Quintet—that incorporate the bass into the ensemble. The great Koussevitzky, who was a bass virtuoso in his native Russia before he became a virtuoso conductor, wrote a few pieces of minor interest and stimulated others to compose for him.

Otherwise? Gary Karr has solved the problem by becoming the outstanding virtuoso of his day. Not long out of Juilliard, he launched a spectacular career for himself, and won praise from even the most skeptical critics. As a result, he has been single-handedly responsible for a major increase in the bass repertory. Hans Werner Henze, Alec Wilder, Malcolm Arnold, Gunther Schuller—these are among the major composers of our time who have created a repertory for Gary Karr and the small company of fellow solo bassists to perform. In his own corner of the musical world, resounding with the mellow roar of his difficult instrument, Gary Karr is one of those special musicians who makes things happen.

Photographed in Los Angeles, 1986.

Aldo Ciccolini

There is no such thing as an "Italian" school of pianists, as there are Russians, French, Germans, and Americans. Italy has produced a small list of admirable keyboard artists, to be sure, but they are all individualists: the mystic Ferruccio Busoni early in the century, the enigmatic Arturo Benedetti Michelangeli, the intellectual Maurizio Pollini, the refined classicist Maria Tipo later on.

And then there is Aldo Ciccolini, Neapolitan by birth but the most all-embracing of his countryman pianists in terms of his range of interests. He has staked a claim to the whimsical, intensely French music of Erik Satie, most of which he has recorded. On the other hand, he is an incomparable interpreter of the most grandiose, inward, dark-colored music of Franz Liszt—the set of *Poetic and Religious Harmonies,* for example.

Winner, in 1949, of the coveted Jacques Thibaud/Marguerite Long competition, which launched his international career, Ciccolini has never been a limelight-stealing musician. He toured American cities, most successfully, after winning the prize, then stayed away for a quarter-century. His re-emergence, in 1975, was almost like a second grand virtuosic debut, and was widely hailed as such.

Photographed in Los Angeles, 1986.

Andrés Segovia

More than any extroverted jazz musician or folksinger, long before any of them were born in fact, Segovia had brought the guitar into prominence. The arts of Spain had always stressed the individual over the ensemble; what more lonely spectacle could there be than the single musician wrapped around the single, small, portable instrument?

Yet the sight of Segovia on a stage could still a crowd of thousands in such locales as Carnegie Hall or the Los Angeles Music Center. He could turn every space into a place of the most intimate communication. You leaned forward, even from a top-balcony seat, and you became a part of Segovia's unique, intimate art.

He had begun playing in public in 1899, at the age of six, but delayed his formal debut for another ten years. By the 1920s the world's major composers were writing for Segovia—not just small, portable pieces but major concertos as well. At ninety-three he was still playing, still wonderful to see and to hear. Those who knew him well—and he was always wonderfully, warmly approachable—knew that his great art at the guitar stemmed from an over-all love of beauty in all the arts. He could, and did, talk for hours on the perfection of, say, a handsomely carved gemstone that he saw in a photograph. Then he could sit with his guitar, and translate the lapidary perfection of that jewel into his own playing.

I was fortunate in taking these pictures in his last year.

Photographed in Los Angeles, 1986.

Andre Watts

The gods of Public Relations smiled upon Andre Watts from the start. His birth—son of a Hungarian mother and a black G.I. stationed in Germany—made good copy, but that was eclipsed by the young Andre's fast rise. At the Philadelphia Music Academy, at a Philadelphia Orchestra's children's concert at age nine, at a grown-up Philadelphia concert at fourteen, and, most of all, at a Leonard Bernstein televised young-people's concert at sixteen, the star of Andre Watts moved into higher, then higher orbit. A week after that televised Bernstein concert young Watts was rushed into service to replace an ailing pianist at a New York Philharmonic broadcast concert, and the rest, as they say, is history.

Fortunately, for Watts and for the rest of the world, his meteoric rise was followed by an ongoing demonstration that here, in this slender, handsome young musician, was a genuine talent. He won his place quickly, but when it came time, in 1988, to celebrate the twenty-fifth anniversary of that spectacular New York debut, Andre Watts was still at, or close to, the top of the heap. He has remained the stunning virtuoso; the technical brilliance of Liszt and Tchaikovsky bring out more of his art than, say, the Beethoven sonatas. But Yale University doesn't dole out its honorary doctorates to mere flash-in-the-pan musical showoffs, and Dr. Andre Watts remains today one of our most skilful, as well as brainiest, keyboard artists.

Photographed in Los Angeles, 1986.

Isaac Stern

Photographed with Yefim Bronfman in Los Angeles, 1986.
Photographed with Kurt Sanderling and the Los Angeles Philharmonic in Los Angeles, 1986.
Photographed in Los Angeles, 1986.

Yefim Bronfman

Born in Israel, handsome, serious Yefim Bronfman found himself enmeshed in the American music-making scene almost before he could speak a word of English. That happened at the renowned Marlboro Music Festival, to which he had been invited on the strength of his prowess as a chamber music performer. That, of course, is Marlboro's strength; although the typical Marlboro man (or woman) may be a striking solo virtuoso (or virtuosa), the emphasis there is on the performer who can blend talents with colleagues, in an exploration of the subtle intricacies of the chamber repertory.

Like many before him—Peter Serkin, Murray Perahia, Richard Goode among others—Bronfman has proven himself imbued with the Marlboro spirit. He has toured as colleague—more than mere accompanist—with the likes of Isaac Stern. He has performed as a member of a trio, formed at Aspen with his colleagues "Jimmy" Lin and Gary Hoffman. And he has maintained a successful virtuoso career as well, in finger-busting works like the Prokofiev Third Piano Concerto as well as the subtler, softer-spoken concertos of Mozart.

He says, in fact, that his experience as a chamber musician has helped him through the demands of the big orchestral works. It's a rare artist who can exert that degree of intelligence in his work.

Photographed with Isaac Stern in Los Angeles, 1986.
Photographed in Los Angeles, 1986.

Janos Starker

Veteran record collectors remember it well: their first experience with an unknown work played by an unknown performer on one of the more obscure LP labels. The work was the Sonata for Unaccompanied Cello by Hungary's Zoltan Kodaly, spellbinding music made even more so by the stupendous musician involved in its performance.

Janos Starker had emigrated to the U.S. from his native Hungary in 1948, became first cellist of the Dallas Symphony that year, moved on to the Metropolitan Opera a year later, and to the Chicago Symphony in 1953. All the while, however, he had been considering the career of a solo cellist, and the phenomenal reception accorded his 1952 recording of the Kodaly Sonata (on the Period label) strengthened his resolve.

Starker's service to music has ranged over a wide repertory. He was among the first to perform the Bach Cello Suites with an authentic cello and bow of Bach's time; in addition he has continued to cultivate composers of his own time—including his countryman Kodaly, but also including Shostakovich and Peter Mennin. Admirably, in the ranks of the world-class virtuosos, Starker also devotes a great deal of his time to teaching, and has for thirty years been on the faculty of the University of Indiana at Bloomington.

Photographed in Costa Mesa, 1986.

Valery Afanasieff

Born in Moscow in 1947, living in Western Europe since 1974, Valery Afanassiev is best known in this country as a collaborator at the piano with the splendid violinists Henryk Szeryng and Gidon Kremer. But that is only a small part of his versatility; his solo recordings of Brahms and Liszt and his fame as a proponent of difficult new music (including the music of the American George Crumb, which requires the pianist to shout, sing and whistle while playing!) fill in the picture of Afanasieff as one of the most able musicians of his time.

His early teachers, at the Moscow Conservatory, included Emil Gilels and Yakov Zak, and his early fame brought him tour dates with the Moscow and Leningrad Philharmonics. To add further luster, he won first prize at the Leipzig Bach competition in 1970, and was a winner in the Queen Elisabeth Competition in Brussels two years later.

Since settling in Western Europe, Afanasieff has appeared frequently in Germany, England, The Netherlands, Japan and the U.S. His programs at most appearances demonstrate his passion for keyboard music of the distant past—including, of course, Bach—and for the adventurous present as well. In addition, his work as a composer has produced at least one work of some fame: *The Encore,* for piano, tape-recorder, several comedians, a little girl, and a dog. His accomplishments don't stop there, however; he has published two successful novels of which the second, *The Fall of Babylon,* was written in English.

The Russian pianist was giving a recital in Pasadena with violinist Gidon Kramer. Practicing a solo piece he was to perform later that evening, he worked methodically; his expression was dour and unchanging. I waited a long time for a change and nothing happened, so after an especially brilliant passage I shouted, in a very loud voice, "BRAVO," and he broke into the broad smile I captured.

Photographed in Pasadena, 1986.

Wynton Marsalis

In 1983 Wynton accomplished the outstanding feat of pulling down Grammy awards both as a jazz trumpeter and for a recording of Baroque trumpet concertos played in the authentic manner. That's the remarkable thing about Wynton Marsalis: his ability to operate freely on both sides of the musical fence and, in doing so, to break down the fence itself. That's a job that needs doing; the artificial boundary that exists in some people's minds between so-called "serious" and "popular" music is as unrealistic a barrier as was the Berlin Wall.

Born in New Orleans in 1961, Wynton Marsalis was recognized for his musicianship as early as age seventeen, when he was singled out at the Berkshire Music Center at Tanglewood as the school's most gifted trumpet player. His double life began at that point: studies at Juilliard, a gig at the Jazz Festival in Montreux, Switzerland, work with Miles Davis and with his own Quintet (which included his saxophone-playing brother, Branford), and a long list of recordings of masterpieces from the Baroque and Classic trumpet repertory.

He is, therefore, one of those rare musicians who can function as a superb entertainer and still maintain respect for a broad spectrum of musical styles.

Photographed in Los Angeles, 1986.

Maurice André

The coal industry's loss is music's gain. Maurice André had spent many of his boyhood years as an apprentice in a coal mine in the south of France, where his father also worked. But the elder André was also an amateur musician in his off hours, and son Maurice followed in those footsteps as well. By the time he was twenty he had pulled down a Prix d'Honneur at his local music school, had moved to Paris and joined the French Radio Orchestra, and was also active in jazz groups. Some prizes—including a competition at Geneva and the International German Radio Competition—helped to speed him along his path.

André's major success was partially the result of superb timing. America's music lovers in the early 1960s were caught up in the wholesale revival of the Baroque concerto repertory, particularly the works of the Italians Vivaldi, Torelli, and Albinoni, and their many confrères. These composers turned out a large and mellow repertory for solo trumpet, much of it highly virtuosic and involving stratospheric tones that got the soloist up into the most brilliant trumpet register. A master of those particular top tones, André developed an ardent following among record collectors.

When last counted, he had made over 250 recordings, most of it dedicated to this Baroque repertory but also including modern concertos composed for André himself. They continue to figure among the top-selling recordings on all the charts.

Photographed in Los Angeles, 1986.

A Tribute to Jascha Heifetz

Photo montage poster of Jascha Heifetz at the Hollywood Bowl in 1985. Done in collaboration with David Hockney.

James Arkatov in collaboration with David Hockney

Chamber Music/LA 1988

Josef Suk

The bloodlines are in order; grandfather Josef Suk, an eminent composer in his own right (a charming Serenade for Strings is justly popular) was in his turn the son-in-law of Antonin Dvorak. The younger Suk was born in Prague in 1929, began studies on the violin at an early age, and made his professional debut, in Prague, at the age of eleven. Undoubtedly he was also raised on recordings of his illustrious grandfather, who in addition to his life as a composer was also a noted violinist and leader of an illustrious string quartet.

The younger Suk also followed the chamber music bent, forming a trio of fellow Czech musicians in the 1950s and, later, playing in the U.S. with the pianist Julius Katchen and cellist Janos Starker. At the same time, his work as a soloist brought him considerable acclaim. A quiet, serious musician—in a manner that might easily be identified as Central European—Suk has been heard in the U.S. in many distinguished performances, mostly of the classic repertory. It is typical of his background and musical leanings that his American debut, in January, 1964, was with the Cleveland Orchestra—whose conductor, the late George Szell, had built it into the idealized Central European orchestra. The young violinist must have felt at home in such surroundings.

Photographed in Los Angeles, 1986.

Albert Goldberg

He saw the greatest of them, and saw through them as well. Albert Goldberg wrote music criticism for the *Los Angeles Times* for forty-two years—from his arrival from his native Midwest in 1947, until he finally laid down his pen in 1989. More than any music critic you can name, Goldberg was in love with the profession he practiced so well. When, after eighteen years as chief critic for the *Los Angeles Times*, his time for retirement came around, he graciously relinquished his post to his successor, Martin Bernheimer, and immediately requested that he be kept on. There was nothing else in the world he wanted to do.

He began in Los Angeles when Jascha Heifetz was the reigning musical celebrity. He presided over the building and opening of the Los Angeles Music Center, and over the rise of the Philharmonic's brash young conductor Zubin Mehta. His last-ever review, in fact, was a commentary on Mehta's Los Angeles concert with the Israel Philharmonic.

Bald, slow-moving, somewhat bent with his ninety-plus years, Goldberg was a familiar sight at the Music Center, even on nights when he was merely in the audience as a spectator. You could always find him at intermission, at the center of a large group of friends and well-wishers. For a critic, not known for the mildness of his manner in his published works, to hold on to that many friends was in itself a rare achievement. But Albert Goldberg was a rare individual.

Photographed in Los Angeles, 1987.

Yehudi Menuhin

The fund of memories is deep and rich: the prodigy who conquered a New York audience at the age of nine; who played concertos of Bach, Beethoven, and Brahms—on one program!—at thirteen; whose recording, at sixteen, of Sir Edward Elgar's Violin Concerto, with Sir Edward conducting, remains unchallenged by any later performance; whose chamber-music performances, especially those with his sister Hephzibah, were the sort to make strong men weak; who returned to England in 1963, to found an extraordinary school for gifted youngsters and receive an honorary knighthood from Queen Elisabeth II; who, after all this, has most recently become a most eloquent and devoted father.

There is enough in the life of Yehudi Menuhin to furnish several biographies; in his case, it isn't only a matter of what he has accomplished, but of how well he has accomplished it all. Other violinists may have surpassed the fund of pure passion he brought to his work; none have touched the level of sheer intelligence and affection on which he has always operated. The most modest of musicians, and one of the wisest, Menuhin has been an honorable adornment to the century lucky enough to contain his accomplishments.

At a concert in 1988, Yehudi Menuhin was both soloist and conductor of the orchestra. During the dress rehearsal I noted a remarkable difference between his approach to conducting, which was relaxed and joyful, and his approach to playing the violin, which I was able to capture in my photographs.

Filmed in Santa Ana, 1986.

Lorin Maazel

Those of us with long memories will remember eleven-year-old Lorin Maazel making his debut as conductor of the formidable NBC Symphony. Maazel had already enchanted observers with his skill as an infant prodigy—on the violin at age five, at the piano two years later.

However, we better remember Maazel for his prodigious adult career on two continents (sometimes almost simultaneously): at the head of the Berlin State Opera, then the Cleveland Orchestra, then the Vienna State Opera, lately the Pittsburgh Symphony.

Admirers will note the sureness of his no-nonsense stick technique; they will admire a remarkable sense of propulsion in his best performances. He leans toward the romantic repertory, but has rescued many an over-written, self-indulgent piece within that repertory from the excesses wished upon it by others. His recorded Sibelius and Tchaikovsky—all the symphonies, in both cases—constitute an object lesson in sane, intelligent conducting.

Between his conducting careers, Lorin, who was a very fine violinist, formed a string quartet, of which I was the celllist. We participated in series of chamber music concerts in Pittsburgh.

Photographed in Santa Ana, 1987.

Minoru Nojima

Slender, shy in demeanor, more scholarly than virtuosic in appearance, Minoru Nojima doesn't cut much of a figure at the piano—until, that is, he starts to play. Then you know immediately why a growing band of Nojima enthusiasts proclaim him the greatest pianist currently active. After an evening of his glowing, deeply rewarding work at the piano, it's hard to believe otherwise.

He first came to prominence in the U.S. as the silver medalist in the 1969 Van Cliburn International Piano Competition. Now there is sometimes a jinx that hovers above Cliburn winners; a surprising number have slid into obscurity—including, you might say, the gold medalist in Nojima's year, Cristina Ortiz. But Nojima himself remains an exception. Without a lot of press agentry, and with a surprisingly small recorded repertory, he has slowly and surely built an impressive career. He was, by the way, the first Cliburn laureate—and, so far, the only one—invited back in a later competition to serve as judge (in 1985, and again in 1989).

His programs aren't always very iconoclastic; he sticks pretty much to the classics and the Impressionists. But he can play the C-major Sonata of Mozart, the one everybody learns in piano lessons, and uncover deep and beautiful elements beneath the surface. At the other end of the spectrum, he can draw colors out of, say, the suite of *Miroirs* of Ravel that might astound even that color-conscious composer.

Photographed in Los Angeles, 1987.

Ruggero Ricci

The Riccis of San Francisco were a prodigiously talented brood. Six of Ruggero's siblings were aimed toward a musical career in their early days, and three of them made it all the way: Ruggero himself, his cellist brother George and the violinist sister Emma. Like other prodigies nurtured in San Francisco—among them Yehudi Menuhin and Isaac Stern—Ruggero himself also made an early start, with a debut concert at the age of ten with his teacher, the legendary Louis Persinger, assisting at the piano.

Like all too few prodigies from the time, however, Ruggero matured into a noble musician. By the age of twenty he had some sixty concertos in his repertoire; these included not only the familiar repertory but a number of new works created for him. He also delved into the literature of the past, and unearthed some long-lost concerto material by Paganini that richly deserved reentry onto the public stage.

Above all, Ricci became a serious and dedicated musical explorer. His recitals and recordings of music for violin alone—including the notoriously difficult Bartok Sonata along with the powerful works of Bach—were among the sovereign musical experiences of the 1960s.

Photographed in Santa Ana, 1987.

Yo-Yo Ma

America first began to notice Yo-Yo Ma in the early 1970s, when the small, serious moppet—barely out of his teens—took the Carnegie Hall stage to play chamber music alongside such grizzled veterans as Isaac Stern and Leonard Rose. Could such things be? In the seemingly omnipotent hands of the young man, born in Paris of Chinese parentage, they could.

He's a phenomenon, that smiling, soft-spoken musician, still boyish in countenance into his thirties. He takes musical chances: programs of nothing but the unaccompanied Suites of Bach are not, after all, calculated to set an audience's toes to tapping. The brain power behind that powerful bowing arm, however, is assurance enough. Even in these days when we seem to be fairly well-stocked with cellists, Yo-Yo Ma is exceptional.

Not content with the existent cello repertory, he has lately taken to commissioning new works—with striking results. At Tanglewood in the summer of 1989, he introduced a concerto composed for him by H. K. Gruber, the Austrian composer who claims descent from the composer of "Silent Night." A wild piece it was, but our young cellist rode it manfully. It did not, however, make for a particularly silent night.

I was photographing Yo-Yo Ma at a master class when he was illustrating different ways of holding the cello. I caught him as he was playfully exaggerating the playing stance of Mstislav Rostropovitch by holding his cello almost horizontally. (Rostropovitch holds his cello in a much more vertical position than many cellists.)

Photographed in Los Angeles, 1988.

Jean-Pierre Rampal

The flute seems to be the quintessential French instrument. Mozart wrote his only solo music for that instrument during his visit to Paris; even before Mozart's time, however, it was a favored instrument in reams of Baroque chamber music.

That repertory might still be gathering dust, however, but for the yeoman work in our own century of a number of noble flutists. First there was the Moyse family, some of them still active at Rudolf Serkin's Marlboro Music Festival in Vermont. And then there is Rampal.

It's an amazing but common sight: a large hall—Manhattan's Carnegie, for example—sold-out to the rafters, its capacity audience mesmerized by the slender tones of Rampal's flute. But it happens. Like Casals with the cello or Segovia with the guitar, Rampal has explored a world of expression, an infinity of shading of his tone, so that the flute stands forth as a new and marvelous sound experience.

He hails from Marseilles, studied medicine for a time before dedicating his life to music. Until Rampal, flute recitals tended to attract only other flutists; Rampal has changed that dramatically. In his time, such composers as Poulenc and Jolivet have composed for him. The French flute, in the French hands of Rampal, continues strong.

Photographed in Los Angeles, 1990.

Nikolai Petrov

Nikolai Petrov was born into a family of musicians and dancers famous throughout Russia. He displayed unusual talent at an early age, trained with Yakov Zak at the Moscow Conservatory, and took prizes at the Van Cliburn and the Queen Elisabeth Competitions.

In 1986, following the signing of the U.S.-Soviet Cultural Exchange Agreement, Petrov was invited to perform with the New York Philharmonic. The first Soviet artist to appear under the new exchange agreement, he made a highly successful orchestral debut and has since returned many times to America.

His international touring over the past twenty years has included Eastern and Western Europe, Asia, the United Kingdom, North and South America, and the Soviet Union.

Photographed in Pasadena, 1987.

Andrea Lucchesini

There is a certain mystique that surrounds musicians from Italy that sets them apart. Perhaps it's the beauty of their homeland, perhaps the exquisite range of flavorings in its food; perhaps it's as simple as the theory that Italians, above all others, think in melody. Three generations, at least, of Italian artistic outlook are represented in this selection of musicians at work, from Castelnuovo-Tedesco and Toscanini to Ciccolini and beyond. Andrea Lucchesini is the youngest of our Italians, but he carries his country's musical language in his own heart as well.

Born in Montecatini—a region famous for its health-giving natural waters—in 1965, Lucchesini went for his major pianistic training to the great Maria Tipo, virtuosa and teacher, and rounded off his studies at the Verdi Institute in Ravenna. In 1983 he became the first native to win his country's prestigious Dino Ciani Piano Competition in Milan, and that win—as these things happen—launched his international career.

Unlike some competition winners, however, Lucchesini—tall, athletic looking, serious in mien—has remained at or near the top. His records—Beethoven Sonatas especially—marked him as a musician of high intelligence and original thinking. When last heard from, he had been tapped to step in for the ailing superstar Jorge Bolet for a recital at Lincoln Center. Those were large shoes to fill, but young Lucchesini is a musician capable of major feats.

Photographed in Los Angeles, 1987.

Nicolas Slonimsky

Call him polymath, call him pixie; Nicolas Slonimsky embodies some of both. Wake him at 2 A.M. to ask for the dates of any musician within the 2,577 pages of his latest edition of Baker's Biographical Dictionary of Musicians, and he will reel them off for you like some user-friendly computer. But Nicolas Slonimsky is no computer; at the age of ninety-six, his powers of mind and memory have been studied by teams from medical colleges—studied, but not necessarily explained.

Not many minutes of those ninety-six years have been frittered away. In the 1920s he came to Boston from his native Russia to help Serge Koussevitzky unravel new scores. Later he himself conducted the first performances of works by Henry Cowell, Edgard Varèse, Charles Ives—the first generation of distinctive American composers. Later on, in a magazine called *Modern Music* (much missed nowadays), he wrote about this music. In the 1930s, hired to conduct the entire season at Hollywood Bowl, he was fired in mid-season for his propagation of new music.

He can, and often will, recreate some of the music of his old buddies: Henry Cowell pieces in which the pianist plays clutching an orange, or whomps down on the keyboard with fist or forearm. His own compositions include an emotional setting of a clutch of advertising slogans. Until you've heard "Children Cry for Castoria" set to music by Nicolas Slonimsky, you ain't heard nothin'.

Nicolas is a charming ninety-six year old pixie who delights in doing things backwards, such as playing the piano with his back to the piano, so I thought it only appropriate to photograph him backwards. When I showed the picture to him, he was delighted.

Photographed in Los Angeles, 1987.

Annie Fischer

Nearly half a century after its outbreak, World War II looms ever larger in musical history as a powerful, tragic point of punctuation. To an artist of Annie Fischer's generation, for example, it meant a hiatus in career-building at a most crucial point.

Fischer was born in Budapest in 1914. Her early studies—most notably, work with Hungary's sovereign piano virtuoso Ernst von Dohnanyi—aimed her at a brilliant career. At nineteen, she had already won first prize in the Franz Liszt Competition in Budapest, back in the days when competitions were few and a big win was a major spur to a career. But then came Hitler and the War, and the career of Annie Fischer, as with many others, had to be put on "hold."

Fischer was more fortunate than most. Recordings after the war—especially a beautiful, spacious performance of the Brahms B-flat Concerto—assured the world that her talent remained unmarred by years of hardship. The fellow Hungarian George Szell brought Annie Fischer to America, for a series of spectacular appearances with the Cleveland Orchestra.

A sober, undemonstrative player, Fischer is part of that European contingent whose best work is in the classic repertory. She has become particularly renowned as a performer of Mozart. An unsensational career hers has truly been, but a deeply satisfying one nonetheless.

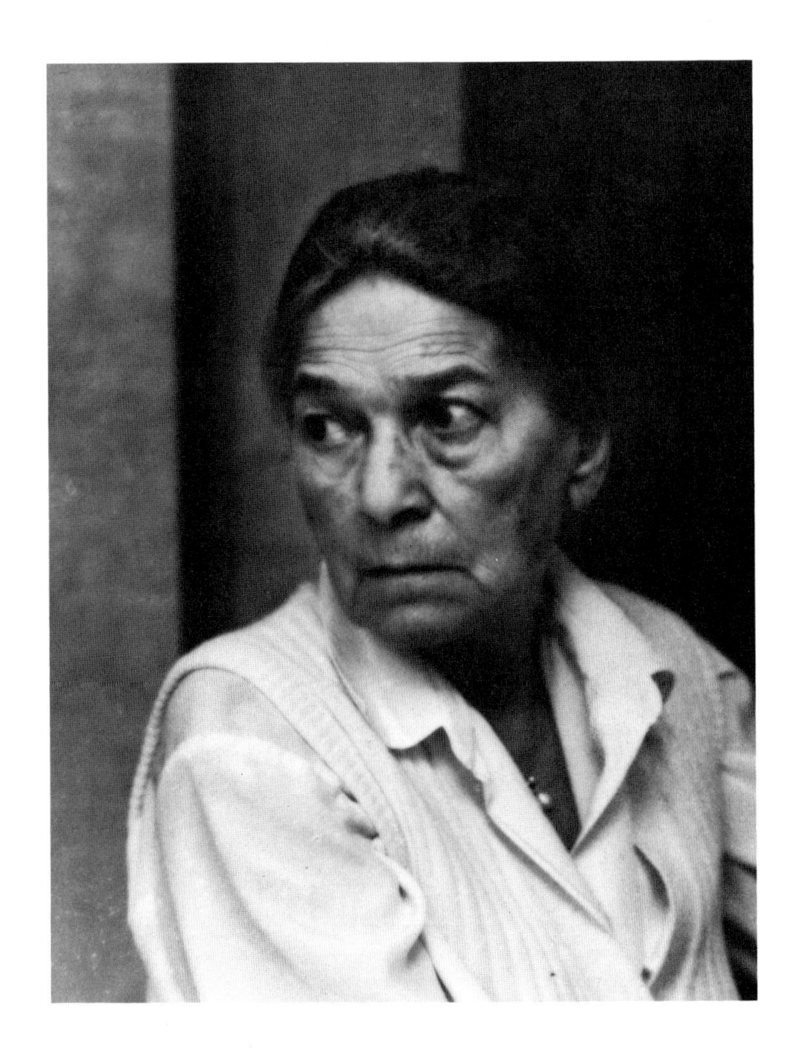

Photographed in Pasadena, 1988.

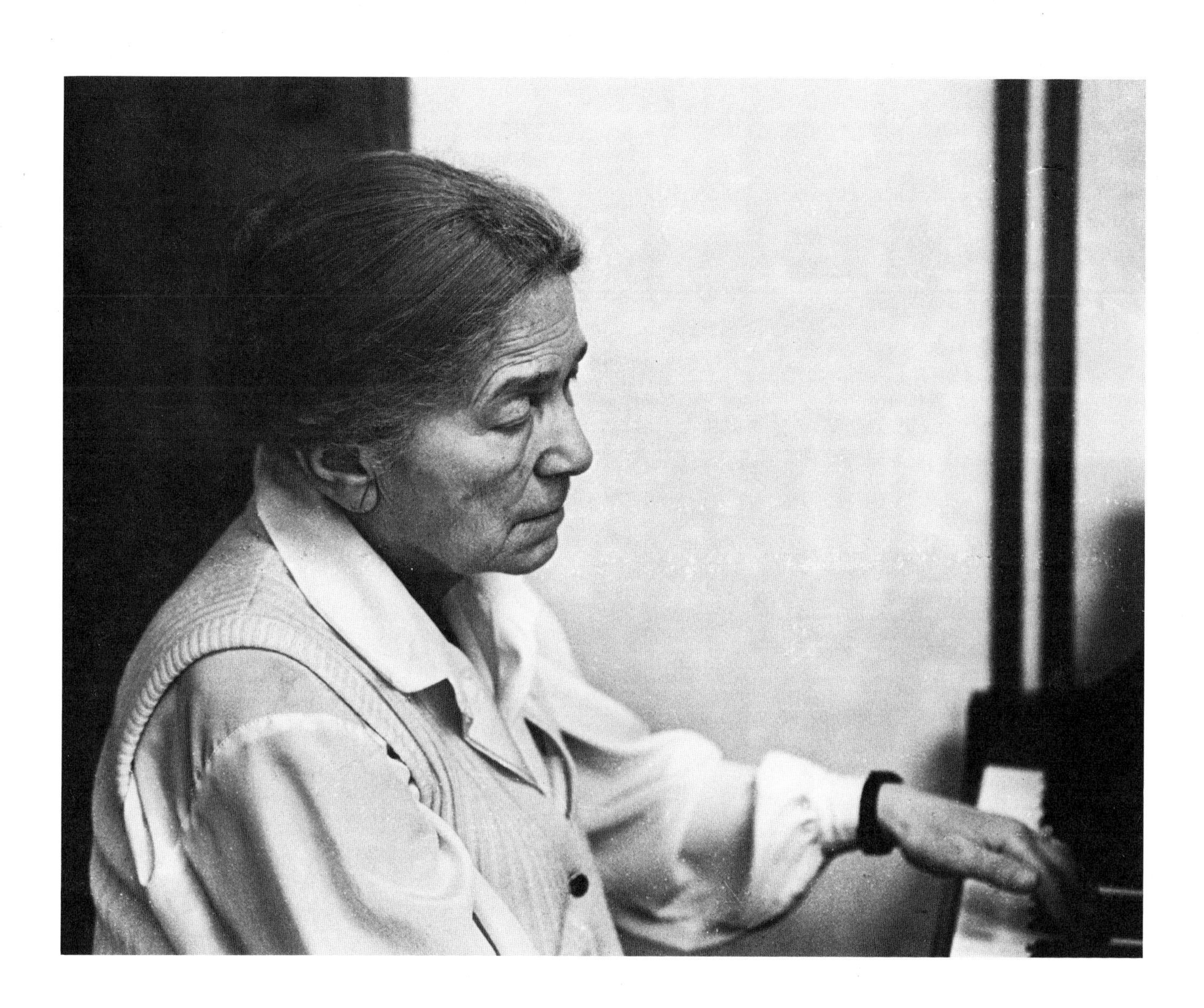

Ravi Shankar

We first learned the name "Shankar" shortly before World War II, when a troupe of Indian dancers and musicians, bearers of an exotic but mostly unknown high art, performed their strange and exquisite repertory before small audiences of connoisseurs. Its leader was Uday Shankar, and in the ensemble was his younger brother, Ravi. Nobody could have guessed at the time that it would be Ravi, years later, who would accomplish the breakthrough and bring the classical art music of India into a place of worldwide high honor.

It remains an exotic art: Ravi at his large, elaborate sitar, drawing out glistening, pulsing sounds that whirl faster and ever faster, all following ages-old patterns of improvisation, with another player tapping out a gentle, steady rhythm on drums and a third player maintaining a steady drone as a harmonic basis. Ravi has played in films—notably in Satyajit Ray's wonderful *Apu* trilogy; he has appeared at new-age and rock concerts. He was at one time a major contributor to the world musical view of the Beatles; Beatle George Harrison journeyed to India to enlist Ravi as guru, and that did no harm to either of their fame.

Now pushing seventy, Ravi Shankar works on tirelessly to bring his country's music into the mainstream without violating its uniqueness. He has composed and played concertos with symphony orchestras; he has taught at major conservatories. He is, in fact, one of our genuinely omnipotent musicians, and no matter that his art clings to its foreignness above all.

Photographed in Pasadena, 1988.

Michael Tilson Thomas

His ancestry is rooted in the arts; the Tomaschevskys were one of the great performing families in New York's famous Yiddish theater at the turn of the century. Michael Tilson Thomas's artistic inclinations were in a somewhat different direction, however.

Not yet twenty, he was already a legend at the University of Southern California's school of music, as a demon pianist and conductor for whom no music however difficult held any fears, and a promising composition student of the much-respected Ingolf Dahl. It was Dahl's influence that earned young Michael a regular berth at the Monday Evening Concerts, that long-established new-music series which regularly attended to new works by Stravinsky, Schönberg and Boulez, among others.

By his mid-twenties Thomas had served as assistant conductor to Pierre Boulez at Bayreuth, won the Koussevitzky Prize at Tanglewood, and been appointed assistant conductor at the Boston Symphony. On October 22, 1969, not yet twenty-five, he encountered the legendary rite of passage, called upon to replace the ailing William Steinberg at a Boston Symphony Concert at Lincoln Center.

The rest has been non-stop history: stints with the Buffalo Philharmonic and the London Symphony, an operatic debut (in, of all exotic choices, Janacek's *Cunning Little Vixen* at the New York City Opera) and, most recently, the formation of the Orchestra of the New World, a youth ensemble based in Miami, already acclaimed for its ability—like that of its conductor, to play anything and play it well.

Photographed in Santa Ana, 1988.

Cho-Liang "Jimmy" Lin

One of the spectacular consequences of the coming of peace to Asia after World War II was the emergence of a whole generation of young musicians. From Japan, from Korea and from the two Chinas they came. We always tended to imagine that the Asian musical esthetics—their employment of scales and harmonies outside common European usage, for example, might preclude the growth of a serious Asian wing in the performance mainstream. But just the opposite has, in fact, taken place.

Enter Cho-Liang (everybody calls him "Jimmy") Lin, born in Taiwan in 1960. Like most young Asian musicians, he was able to find beginning training at home; by the age of ten he had already pulled down a first prize in a Taiwanese young-musicians competition. But then, like his colleagues from Eastern shores, he journeyed elsewhere—first to the rock-ribbed Conservatorium at Sydney in New South Wales, then to Juilliard. Like all young violinists destined for top honors, he earned a scholarship—at fifteen!—to work with the legendary teacher Dorothy DeLay at Juilliard. From there on it was a matter or prizes, engagements, more prizes, and record contracts.

In performance he is anything but an exotic. He has recorded Mozart concertos, whose transparent beauties are the ultimate test of a violinist's best intentions. And he plays them beautifully, does this young Jimmy Lin.

Photographed in Santa Ana, 1988.

Eduardo Mata

The ranks of serious musical heroes out of Mexico are rather slender, but the efforts of Eduardo Mata seem to promise a change for the better. Himself a distinguished composer and conductor, Mata has used his remarkable success in the latter field to earn a fair shake for many of his countrymen; to him we owe a great deal of the growing respect Mexico's serious music has lately earned.

Mata was born in Mexico City in 1942. He studied composition with Carlos Chávez and Julian Orbón, then moved north to work at conducting seminars at the Berkshire Music Center at Tanglewood. For a time he seemingly shuttled across the border, conducting orchestras in Phoenix, Guadalajara, and, currently, Dallas. Well ensconced and much admired on his podium in that Texas metropolis, he has even handcarried his notably conservative Dallas audience toward an understanding of new and newer music—the wilderness of Boulez and Stockhausen, not to mention his own works. He seems, so far, to be getting away with this iconoclasm; more power to him.

Photographed in Santa Ana, 1988.

Jascha Heifetz

Photographed with Brooks Smith in Los Angeles, 1966.
Photographed in Los Angeles, 1966.

Jacob Druckman

The sound of music, to this outstanding American composer, can be many things: aggregations of percussion instruments including primitive drums, the howl and whoosh of electronic sounds, a symphony orchestra throttled down to an exquisite, feathery whisper. Jacob Druckman is one of our best active composers, one of the most versatile and generous.

The generosity comes about, most of all, in the position of leadership he has assumed among his fellows. When the remarkable composers' service organization called "Meet the Composer" set up a residence program, whereby certain creative artists attached themselves to major symphony orchestras, Druckman joined the New York Philharmonic, advised it on the choice of other new music to add to its programs, and organized a yearly series of new-music concerts (called "Horizons") to examine the current state of the musical world. Thus, while some composers prefer to inhabit ivory towers, Druckman became a citizen of the cosmopolitan musical world.

He has taught at Yale, and at the thriving summer festival at Aspen. His own music, however, is not a bit professorial: tough and complex at its core, it also gives off a sense of warm, communicative humanness that has made him one of the most loved and respected musician of his generation. His marvelous, glinting orchestral piece called *Windows* won, and richly deserved, the 1972 Pulitzer Prize in music.

Photographed in Aspen, 1988.

Jan De Gaetani

There are those who would close the books on music at around 1910, forget that Stravinsky ever composed *The Rite of Spring* and reduce today's minimalist composers to an even smaller minimum. New music needs its supporters on both sides: audiences willing to stretch their ears, and performers willing and able to stretch their techniques to accommodate the demands of living composers.

In Jan DeGaetani's all-too-brief career (which ended in the summer of 1989 with her death at fifty-six), she sang Schubert beautifully, sang, and even recorded, Stephen Foster with grace and respect for its simple eloquence. But her great service was to contemporary music. She devoted phenomenal amounts of energy to mastering a composer's complex vocal line that skipped widely from top notes to bottom, that rested on no recognizable harmonic system, that demanded that a singer howl, whistle, gurgle, or half-speak–half-sing, all in the name of originality. She mastered these problems, and she also mastered the way to pass their solutions on to her students.

There were easier ways of developing a singer's career, but Jan DeGaetani loved the road she had taken and achieved that career with honor and distinction. The future of music depends, quite literally, on there being people around to pick up where she left off.

Photographed in Aspen, 1988.

Jorge Mester

He's been around, Jorge Mester. Mexico City was his birthplace—hence the "Jorge"; his parents were Hungarian, hence the "Mester." His education was largely in the U.S., at a military school in Hollywood and, more to the point, at the Juilliard School. There he fell in with a madcap classmate named Peter Schickele, who was in the process of inventing a strange alterego known as P. D. Q. Bach. Mester became the conductor of the first, notoriously memorable concerts of that unseemly collaboration; the records of that event survive.

Later, Mester was to turn serious, and with a vengeance. He led the enterprising Louisville Orchestra for twelve years (1967–79), giving during that time some two hundred first performances, most of them of works commissioned by that remarkable orchestra. Among his other accomplishments: head of the Kansas City Philharmonic (1971–74), of the Aspen Music Festival (1980–1990) and of the Pasadena Symphony (1984 to the present). If that didn't add up to enough activity for one lifetime, Mester can also be found on the faculty at Juilliard, or at home practicing on his violin or viola.

Photographed in Aspen, 1988.

Violine I A
Violine I A

James Galway

An imp, a leprechaun perhaps . . . but also a musician of great skill and flair. James Galway has so much fun just being himself that it's sometimes hard to take him as seriously as he deserves. That face of his, with its hearty smile, is authentic Irish, as much of Galway as his name. He likes to play up the Irish in him, begorrah, by including on his serious, classical concerts an encore or two for his trusty tin whistle. It's amazing what that modest twopenny instrument can accomplish in the master's hands!

Galway was born in Belfast in 1939. He began his studies as a violinist, but changed instruments in boyhood to his first love. By fourteen he had earned a scholarship to study the flute in London, and went on from there to prestigious positions in orchestras at the Stratford-Upon-Avon Shakespeare Festival, the Royal Opera in Covent Garden, the London Symphony and the Royal Philharmonic. At thirty he was ensconced as first flutist in Herbert von Karajan's Berlin Philharmonic, a post he held for six years. At forty he had amassed enough experience to venture on an autobiography.

Galway has devoted himself in recent years to his solo career, which includes performances of music composed for him. One of his real charmers is John Corigliano's concerto called *The Pied Piper,* which calls for, among other things, a chorus of children playing toy flutes, who materialize out of the audience at the end of the piece and follow their hero flutist up the aisles and out of the hall. It's a hoot!

Photographed in Aspen, 1988.

Cecile Licad

The Philippines have not sent many world-class performers into the musical world as yet, but Cecile Licad—born in Manila in 1961—is one of the most promising and, so far, one of the most successful. As a child she studied with Rosario Picazo, and gave her first public concert at the age of seven.

Following the customary trail by talented musicians from smaller countries, she soon made her way to America, and to studies at Philadelphia's Curtis Institute with Rudolf Serkin, Mieczyslaw Horszowski, and Seymour Lipkin. By 1979 she was ready for American conquest, which began at Tanglewood that summer, in a concerto performance with the Boston Symphony. Two years later—again, following the customary pathway for a growing, successful career, she was named gold-medal winner in New York's prestigious Leventritt Award, the same prize that had launched Van Cliburn, among many others, into musical orbit.

Photographed in Pasadena, 1988.

Alexander Slobodyanik

First there were Richter, Gilels, and Ashkenazy; then it seemed as if every other pianist on the treadmill for a major world-class career had come from the Soviet Union. Inevitably, many of them fell by the wayside, even some of the most promising. So far, Alexander Slobodyanik seems likely to survive that initial onrush of momentary fame, and to move on to a major career.

He was born in Kiev, Vladimir Horowitz's home town, in 1941, and followed Horowitz's own pathway to Moscow, where he enrolled at that city's much-honored Conservatory. Although his showing in the 1966 Tchaikovsky Competition was not sensational—it attracted enough attention to launch the twenty-five-year-old pianist on a number of concert tours in the Soviet Union and, later, in Western Europe as well.

Slobodyanik came to America in the 1970s, again to distinguished if qualified acclaim. Critics admired the strength of his fingers, but that's the least one can say about any properly trained Soviet performer. What ravished American audiences the more, with Slobodyanik, was the genuine eloquence of his romantic approach. His career has grown slowly, but it has been a study in growing mastery. Here is a genuinely memorable musician.

Photographed in Pasadena, 1988.

Nicholas McGegan

Along about 1980, the musical world began to stir to the work of a knot of young conductors, most of them centered in London, who were off founding orchestras to play the classical repertory—music of the 17th and 18th centuries, mostly—with instruments authentic to the music's own time, and with a restoration of performance practices of that time. Unlike his colleagues Christopher Hogwood and Trevor Pinnock, Nicholas McGegan wasn't tempted to start his own orchestra; he played, instead, in most of the others—Baroque flute, mostly, and harpsichord.

He soon moved up to the conductor's podium, however, and found himself an area of specialty in the performance of Baroque operas—Monteverdi, Handel, and Rameau in particular. To the diminutive, apple-cheeked McGegan, "authentic performance" means more than merely restoring the right instruments and starting the trills on the right note; it is a matter of restoring the lively spirit of invention that music of all times must have.

Lately, his career has been largely centered on the West Coast. His triumphs include Monteverdi operas in wonderfully imaginative stagings by the enterprising Long Beach Opera, and a fabulous series of concerts and recordings with San Francisco's Philharmonia Baroque Orchestra, which he took over in 1985. No stickler of the early-music-only persuasion, McGegan has also had notable success with Offenbach's *Tales of Hoffmann* at Long Beach and Stravinsky's *The Rake's Progress* with the Washington Opera at Kennedy Center.

Photographed in Pasadena, 1988.

Moura Lympany

What sweet vapors rise from that elegant name! They suggest the pianist devoted to the romantic repertory, and very good at it. Moura Lympany's name first came to America via a recording of the lavishly romantic Piano Concerto of Aram Khatchaturian, one of the earliest triumphs in the onrush of "high fidelity" recordings shortly after World War II.

Lympany, born in 1916, had the normal musical upbringing accorded talented students: Royal Academy, some years in Vienna, then back to finish off in the classes of Tobias Matthay (who also taught Dame Myra Hess). In 1938 she took a second prize at the Ysaye Competition in Brussels, edged out by a brash Soviet newcomer named Emil Gilels.

Although a romanticist by nature (with marvelous recordings of Rachmaninoff, in particular, to establish her claim), Lympany has been a lifelong champion of new music, within certain expressive limits. Her repertory includes the concertos of Fredric Delius, Alan Rawsthorne, and John Ireland; in 1969 she played the concerto of Cyril Scott at the composer's ninetieth birthday celebration; in 1979 she was made a Commander of the British Empire. In 1989, after a long absence from these shores, she once again paid us a loving visit, charming audiences coast-to-coast with her name—and with her music.

Photographed in Pasadena, 1988.

Andras Schiff

Bach on the piano? That may sound like heresy in these times when authentic performances on period instruments are all the rage, yet the young Hungarian Andras Schiff has flown in the face of current taste, and done it with remarkable success. On the London label he has recorded virtually all the major keyboard music of Bach, played with elegance and logic on a contemporary grand piano.

"On whatever instrument we choose to play," Schiff has written, "style is of prime importance. The modern performer should love this music, and should above all have faith in his musical tastes and instincts." It's a fair argument, and Schiff has marshaled potent support for his words in the strength and clarity of his own playing.

Born in Budapest in 1953, Schiff is one of three young Hungarian pianists out to conquer the world; Dezso Ranki and Zoltan Kocsis are the others. Schiff departs from his countrymen, however, in choice of repertory: a classicist above all. In London he studied, interestingly enough, with the harpsichordist George Malcolm. He went on to win a major prize at the 1974 Tchaikovsky Competition, and won England's Leeds Competition the following year: a potent argument that even major contest winners can sometimes entertain leanings toward the classics, and the intelligence to back up their choice with words.

Photographed in Pasadena, 1989.

Lynn Harrell

Lynn Harrell grew up with music; his father was the great American baritone Mack Harrell, beloved for his deep, abiding musicianship over a wide repertory, from Bach Cantatas to the title role in Berg's *Wozzeck*. You could say, therefore, that Lynn Harrell, with his own deep, abiding musicianship applied to the baritone member of the string family, is carrying on his father's work. That is meant as a compliment; like the elder Harrell, the son has become particularly noted for his work in expanding musical horizons.

This he does, first of all, by plunging fearlessly into unfamiliar repertory: newly commissioned concertos alongside forgotten works from the past. But along with his zeal as an apostle of great works for his instrument, Harrell has also become the great cello teacher of his time—at the University of Southern California, where he has headed the cello department for several years, and at the annual Los Angeles Philharmonic Institute, one of this country's foremost summer training programs.

Watching Lynn Harrell play, you get the feeling that he is having the time of his life. His face takes on a sort of beatific expression; his body seems to move with the music as if trying to wring that one last measure of passion out of his instrument. Later he will tell you about playing, and in that hearty, booming baritone voice you hear the embodiment of a sort of idealized cello.

Photographed in Pasadena, 1989.

Lukas Foss

By 1937, when Lukas Foss and his family had emigrated to the United States from their native Germany, he, at fifteen, was already an accomplished musician—pianist, conductor, composer, flutist. Within the next few years his further growth proclaimed him one of the true musical phenomena of his age. In 1945, at twenty-three, he became the youngest musician ever to win a Guggenheim Fellowship. By then his music was being performed in New York and Boston, and Serge Koussevitzky had taken him on as resident pianist with the Boston Symphony.

Foss has never really slowed down. The 1950s found him in Southern California, where he stood at the cutting edge of avant-garde musical life with his UCLA-based Improvisational Ensemble. From that benevolent climate he next braved the chills to found, at the University of Buffalo, another new-music ensemble and a major new-music workshop that attracted composers from all world cultures. Simultaneously, he rebuilt the ailing Brooklyn Philharmonia into a major performing body, again surrounding its activity with a complex of new-music projects.

As a composer, he has likewise moved rapidly. The 1960 *Time Cycle*, a suite for soprano and chamber ensemble using improvisational techniques, won a New York Critics' Circle Award, one of many citations. He has kept abreast, or usually slightly ahead, of major thought processes in the rarefied world of new music; when styles change, Lukas Foss usually gets there first.

Photographed in Los Angeles, 1989.

Alicia de Larrocha

To look at her, you can't imagine how Alicia de Larrocha ever decided to become a pianist in the first place. Her hands are tiny; she can barely manage the interval of a tenth. She, too, is tiny; where, you might ask, does she get the strength for that glorious romp through the Brahms piano concertos, or the wild danceries in the music of her countryman, Enrique Granados, that she plays with supreme abandon?

Well, she gets that strength from somewhere. Her teacher, the legendary Frank Marshall, put her on stretching exercises and they worked. She made her American debut in 1955, but returned immediately to her native Spain. Not until 1962 did she make her American re-entry, and this time it took. Undoubtedly the most popular woman pianist of our time, she can and does sell out houses in New York and Los Angeles several times a year.

Her repertory is vast; she is the queen of Mozart, and her frequent appearances at Lincoln Center's "Mostly Mozart" summer concerts are the crown of her concert career. She plays the poetic Beethoven—the Fourth Concerto, for example—more beautifully than you'd believe possible, but also musters the strength to face down the titanic "Emperor."

Then there is that Spanish repertory: insinuating, haunting—small-scale perhaps, but cut like small diamonds. De Larrocha restored the piano pieces of Albéniz and Granados to respectability, after generations of lesser musicians had used them for filler material. She is one of music's masters, and one of its saviors as well.

Photographed in Los Angeles, 1989.

Kazuhito Yamashita

The music of Japan quivers with the delicate sounds of plucked instruments—the koto most of all—but Kazuhito Yamashita is another kind of phenomenon, a guitarist of international virtuoso status who revels in music that others might fear to touch. Imagine, for example, the warm orchestral colors of Dvorak's *New World* Symphony turned into a showpiece for a solo guitarist! Can't be done, you say? Then you haven't heard Yamashita.

Born in 1961, Yamashita first took up the guitar at the age of eight. By thirteen, after working with the Spanish master Narciso Yepes, he was ready to step into Japanese concert life, with recitals in Nagasaki and Tokyo. More lessons followed, including a master class with the great Segovia; in 1976 Yamashita walked away with a competition sponsored by the Japanese Federation of Guitarists. A year later he had won similar prizes in France and Switzerland.

From then to now, Yamashita's career has been an endless round of competition wins and sold-out recitals. Mastering the traditional guitar repertory at an early age, he moves on now to assimilating the symphonic literature. How far can he go? Wagner's *Ring of the Nibelung*, perhaps, transcribed for Yamashita's solo guitar? Don't sell him short!

Photographed in Los Angeles, 1989.

Heinrich Schiff

Cellists in this era seem as plentiful as—well, as violinists did a couple of decades ago. Nobody knows why these things happen; fortunately, the sound of the cello is so ravishing, the music composed for it so satisfying, that there is always room at the top. Currently that room is occupied by the likes of Yo-Yo Ma, Lynn Harrell, the very young Matt Heimovitz, Mstislav Rostropovich, and Heinrich Schiff.

Schiff is Austria's entry into the ranks. He was born in 1951 in the town of Gmunden, beloved by Franz Schubert as a rustic vacation spot. His early years as a virtuoso were marked by a series of competition awards—nothing but the best, in Geneva, Vienna, and Warsaw. He has gone everywhere: to Australia, to Japan, eventually to the U.S., where he now tours regularly.

A jovial, roundish man, Schiff might be said to look the way his instrument sounds: full and mellow. On recordings he has already accounted for much of the cream of the cello repertory: the Bach Suites, the Dvorak Concerto and the two of Haydn, a strong novelty in the Concerto by Witold Lutoslawski. An immensely satisfying performer—without the panache of a Rostropovich, perhaps, but with a quiet, deep wisdom that shapes his immaculate sense of the phrase—Heinrich Schiff demands, and merits our attention.

Photographed in Los Angeles, 1989.

Aprille Millo

You hear it on all sides: like the heroines in grand opera, opera itself is languishing. Where are the stars? the cry goes up; where, indeed, are those larger-than-life creatures with the deep throats, whose interpretations and whose vocal prowess could lend an aura of magic to that exotic and irrational art known as opera.

Right now the hopes for a return of pure, magical operatic glamor rest on a young woman hardly out of her twenties, born and raised in Los Angeles but already the toast of the operatic world. Aprille Millo attended Hollywood High while her ambitious parents saw to her musical grooming. She sang with some local companies around Los Angeles, while the fame of her budding talent spread by that peculiar underground that sees to the spread of operatic information faster than any printing press ever could.

In New York, Millo made her way, slowly, toward the Metropolitan Opera. She made herself available for a wide selection of repertory to the conductor Eve Queler, who put on concert performances of grand opera in Carnegie Hall. She sang to European audiences, at the marvelously larger-than-life summer performances at Verona's Arena and Rome's Baths of Caracalla. She got her picture on the cover of operatic fan magazines, where the pure-voice aficionados argued the superiority of the Millo of today versus, say, the Zinka Milanov of yesterday. She has, in short, arrived.

Photographed in Los Angeles, 1989.

Pierre Boulez

Igor Stravinsky and Arnold Schönberg were the dominate figures in the first half of this century, controlling by the exertion of their own creative imagination the direction of musical thinking on a broad front. By the same token, and to the same degree, Pierre Boulez has been the dominant figure of the century's second half.

He is a curious sort of dominator, this unimposing figure, dressed like a provincial businessman, soft-spoken and friendly to the slightest approach. But he has, in his time, forced a new way of thinking about music—the creation of it, and the recreation through performance—even on that part of the musical world that resists him utterly.

In his seven stormy years as conductor of the New York Philharmonic, whatever you might say about his interpretations or programming, he raised the level of performance to an almost superhuman level, all thanks to his phenomenal ear and impeccably clear beat. As the founder and director of IRCAM, the Paris-based studio for research into electronic musical resources, he pushed back the horizons for generations of young composers, and even envisioned a new way of designing listening space. As a composer himself, he has defined for our time the nature of musical expressivity.

Paris and Los Angeles are the antipodes of his existence; he flourishes in both. The Los Angeles Philharmonic plays under his leadership with a clarity and strength that no other conductor currently can produce. Seventy miles north at Ojai, a rustic paradise where Boulez appears to lead a unique festival every two or three years, this most complex of today's musical creators is, among the town's ranchers and orange-growers, a local hero.

Photographed in Los Angeles, 1989.

Neeme Jarvi

The small republic of Estonia, locked in its struggle for political freedom, has not hitherto been particularly well known for its output of world-class musicians. Currently, however, two of its expatriates well deserve that description. One is the composer Arvo Pärt, whose subtle mystical works—most of them for small ensemble—have attracted a band of fanatical admirers. The other is the conductor Neeme Jarvi. Interestingly enough, both men emigrated out of Estonia on the same day in 1980, both despairing of the future of artistic freedom in that isolated land.

Jarvi had been the conductor of Estonia's one major orchestra, and a pupil at one time of Leningrad's great Eugen Mravinsky. Now, in the West, he has built a second career, and a most distinguished one: music director of the splendid orchestra at Sweden's Göteborg, principal guest conductor with the Scottish National, and a frequent visitor to the United States. His official residence, in fact, is currently in New Jersey.

He excels in the warm, robust symphonic repertory; his recorded Dvorak and Strauss are among the finest performances those composers have ever received. He is, at the same time, an ardent proponent of new music, including that of his countryman Pärt. A hearty, jovial man who has the power to make instant friends of every symphony orchestra he visits, Jarvi has quietly taken his place as one of the great conductors of our time.

Photographed in Los Angeles, 1989.

Midori

Handing the 1989 Dorothy B. Chandler Award to the eighteen-year-old Midori at the Los Angeles Music Center's twenty-fifth anniversary gala, Zubin Mehta referred to her as the "Jascha Heifetz of the 21st Century." That's an enormous burden to place upon such tender shoulders, but the young Osaka-born whiz kid just might deserve such trust.

She began her violin studies with her mother at age four. Four years later a tape of her playing found its way to the Juilliard School's renowned teacher Dorothy DeLay; at age ten Midori became DeLay's student, and enrolled as well in master classes by Pinchas Zukerman. In 1982 she auditioned for Zubin Mehta and the New York Philharmonic; Mehta immediately invited her to be the "surprise mystery guest" soloist at the orchestra's New Year's Eve concert. Her performance that night drew a standing ovation from a capacity crowd of New York holiday celebrators.

In 1989 the small virtuosa with the extraordinary bow arm was honored by the Japanese government as the Best Artist of the Year, the youngest person ever to receive such an award.

Photographed in Los Angeles, 1989.

Radu Lupu

In at least one respect, Radu Lupu is a genuine rarity among virtuoso musicians of his time: a competition winner (many times over, in fact) who then went on to fulfill all the promises those victories prophesied. Born in Galati, Romania, in 1945, Lupu earned, early on, a scholarship to study at the Moscow Conservatory, which served as a launching pad to his international career. In short order he won the Van Cliburn Competition in 1966, the Enesco Competition (named after his great violinist/composer/conductor countryman) in 1967, and the highly regarded Leeds Competition in 1969.

Despite his Cliburn win, Lupu returned to his Moscow teachers for another three years. His actual American debut was with the Cleveland Orchestra in 1972. He won immediate praise for his grand, oratorical performance style: a true romanticist at a time when the breed seemed to be dying out. His many records bear out these initial impressions; they include some fiery, sweeping renditions of Brahms piano works, and a loving, original approach to the well-worn concertos of Schumann and Grieg.

He also, however, has performed well in the service of new music; in 1975 he gave the world premiere of yet another Tchaikovsky Piano Concerto—this one by Boris Tchaikovsky (no relation), dedicated by the composer to this splendid Romanian virtuoso.

Photographed in Los Angeles, 1990.

Emanuel Ax

The sight of Emanuel Ax at the piano conjures up one kind of image: serious, scholarly, perhaps a shade ungiving. The sound of Emanuel Ax at the piano, however, is something entirely different. Perhaps this Polish-born virtuoso cuts a less than graceful figure on stage; his playing supplies the full measure of grace, along with power and passion.

Winner, in 1974, of the Arthur Rubinstein Competition, Ax has appeared regularly with practically every major American orchestra, and recorded large chunks of the virtuoso repertory, including some of the most eloquent records of Chopin since Rubinstein's own heyday. Yet he is equally admired as a chamber-music performer, for his frequent appearances in the famous noon-time concerts at the Festival of Two Worlds at Spoleto and at that other chamber-music haven, the Marlboro Music Festival, as well. He appears frequently, and has also recorded, as part of a trio, with the violinist Young-Uck Kim and the cellist Yo-Yo Ma; Ax-Kim-Ma, an easy name to fit onto a concert-hall marquée!

In 1979 Emanuel Ax added a further laurel to his credits, as a winner of the highly regarded Avery Fischer Prize, given by the donor of one of Lincoln Center's several music halls.

Photographed in Los Angeles, 1990.

Erich Leinsdorf

His American debut came at the tender age of twenty-five, and he's been going strong ever since. No, it isn't Leonard Bernstein this time; five years before Bernstein struck that famous blow on behalf of youth on the podium, there was Erich Leinsdorf at the Metropolitan Opera, with the awesome Kirsten Flagstad on the stage in Wagner's *Die Walküre*. He was noticed; "he knew what he wanted from the orchestra, and how to get it," wrote Lawrence Gilman in the *New York Herald Tribune*.

Orchestral mastery; that has, indeed, been the quality most associated with the Viennese-born Leinsdorf over his long career. Whatever the secret that makes an aggregation of players into a smooth ensemble whenever he's on the podium, it's a secret he willingly shares with younger generations, as teacher (notably at the Berkshire Music Festival at Tanglewood) and in his eloquent writings.

On the podium, Leinsdorf is an arresting sight: small in stature, but with arms that seem able to reach the whole expanse of the stage. He is at his best in the repertory of his native Central-Europe, but ventures widely in his programming. His versatility is astounding in all regards, for that matter: at home as much in opera as on the concert stage, in a knotty contemporary composition as in a Mozart symphony. It's safe to say, in fact, that in the half-century since that illustrious debut, he has been more in evidence than any other conductor of this era.

Photographed in Los Angeles, 1990.

Portraits by Alexander Arkatov, 1889-1962

Paul Robeson, *circa* 1930.
Gregor Piatigorsky, *circa* 1932.

Sergei Rachmaninoff, circa 1935.

Isaac Stern at age fifteen.

San Francisco String Quartet (from left to right): Naoum Blinder (Isaac's teacher), Lajos Fenster, Willem Dehe (my teacher), and Nathan Firestone, circa 1935.

ARKATOV
Photo

Afterword
James Arkatov

My interest in photography had an early but roundabout start. My father, Alexander, had a career in the motion picture industry and later on settled in San Francisco where he opened a photography salon in the St. Francis Hotel. There he photographed many of the famous musicians, artists and business people of his day, including Rachmaninoff, Piatigorsky, Ernest Bloch, Diego Rivera, Benjamin Bufano, Erskine Caldwell, Fremont Older and many others. I admired his work and often helped him in the darkroom.

However, before getting into photography seriously, I went through several careers, in music and business.

I started out as a promising young cellist, gave my first solo recital in San Francisco when I was fourteen and a few years later was invited by Fritz Reiner to join the Pittsburgh Symphony.

Ties to San Francisco at that time, however, were quite strong so I returned and joined the San Francisco Symphony under Pierre Monteux for seven years. I then became the principal cellist with the Indianapolis Symphony. After that Fritz Reiner asked me to rejoin the Pittsburgh Symphony, which I did.

While in Pittsburgh, I began taking pictures of the great soloists appearing with the orchestra, such as Fritz Kreisler, Gregor Piatigorsky, Claudio Arrau, Schnabel, Francescatti, Casadesus, and of course Fritz Reiner.

By that time, however, I felt I had had enough of winters in the East and settled in Los Angeles. There I worked in the studios and became principal cellist of the NBC orchestra in Los Angeles.

Continuing my photographic activity while I was on the NBC staff, I photographed Bruno Walter, Jascha Heifetz, Toscanini, Szigeti, Stravinsky, Piatigorsky again, Beecham, Otto Klemperer, and others.

I was invited to join the Hollywood Bowl orchestra for two summers, and there photographed Koussevitsky, Heifetz, Steinberg, Horowitz, Monteux, Leon Fleischer, John Browning, Isaac Stern, Van Cliburn, Arthur Rubinstein, and many others.

Around this time, I was drawn into the business world, joined Pacific Mutual Life Insurance Company, and have remained with them ever since. I developed a successful clientele of business and professional people and worked with them in areas of business insurance, estate and financial planning—as had Charles Ives, composer and insurance agent, a half-century before.

During this period I still took pictures, but less frequently, as I remained very active musically. In 1968 I felt there was a real need for an outstanding chamber orchestra in Los Angeles. Some of my friends put up seed money and I began negotiating with Neville Marriner. A year later, the L.A. Chamber Orchestra had its first successful season. I was its first principal cellist and am very proud that it has developed into a world-class organization.

In recent years, after satisfying careers in music and business, and while still continuing activities in both of these areas, I felt a strong desire to develop (no pun intended) the photographic work that intrigued me for most of my life.

Accordingly, I became more involved in the type of photography that has always interested me, photographing great artists at work, during master classes and at performances.

All these pictures are unposed and only available light was used. Although frequently inadequate, this often added to the mood of the picture. In addition, the intensity of the artists involved in their music-making added further to the unique quality of the photographs.

I found drama and excitement in photographing these artists and hope my photographs convey a degree of those emotions.

Cover and text design by Cyndi Burt.
Typography by Jim Cook.
Printing by Kingsport Press.
Collage by David Hockney.